D0810357

*Bloom's*
# GUIDES

John Steinbeck's
# Of Mice and Men

The Adventures of Huckleberry Finn
All the Pretty Horses
Animal Farm
Beloved
Brave New World
The Chosen
The Crucible
Cry, the Beloved Country
Death of a Salesman
The Grapes of Wrath
Great Expectations
The Great Gatsby
Hamlet
The Handmaid's Tale
The House on Mango Street
I Know Why the Caged Bird Sings
The Iliad
Lord of the Flies
Macbeth
Maggie: A Girl of the Streets
The Member of the Wedding
Of Mice and Men
1984
One Hundred Years of Solitude
Pride and Prejudice
Ragtime
Romeo and Juliet
The Scarlet Letter
Snow Falling on Cedars
A Streetcar Named Desire
The Things They Carried
To Kill a Mockingbird

*Bloom's*
# GUIDES

## John Steinbeck's
# Of Mice and Men

Edited & with an Introduction
By Harold Bloom

**CHELSEA HOUSE**
**P U B L I S H E R S**
An imprint of Infobase Publishing

**Bloom's Guides: Of Mice and Men**

Copyright © 2006 by Infobase Publishing
Introduction © 2006 by Harold Bloom

Chelsea House
An imprint of Infobase Publishing
132 West 31st Street
New York NY 10001

**Library of Congress Cataloging-in-Publication Data**
John Steinbeck's Of mice and men / Harold Bloom, editor.
    p. cm. — (Bloom's guides)
  Includes bibliographical references and index.
  ISBN 0-7910-8581-3
  1. Steinbeck, John, 1902-1968. Of mice and men. I. Title: Of mice and men.
II. Bloom, Harold. III. Series.
  PS3537.T3234O46 2006
  813'.52—dc22                                    2005038038

Chelsea House books are available at special discounts when purchased in bulk
quantities for businesses, associations, institutions, or sales promotions. Please call
our Special Sales Department in New York at (212) 967-8800 or (800) 322-8755.

You can find Chelsea House on the World Wide Web at
http://www.chelseahouse.com

Contributing Editor: Gabriel Welsch
Cover design by Takeshi Takahashi

Printed in the United States of America

Bang EJB 10 9 8 7 6 5 4 3 2 1

This book is printed on acid-free paper.

All links and web addresses were checked and verified to be correct at the time of
publication. Because of the dynamic nature of the web, some addresses and links
may have changed since publication and may no longer be valid.

# Contents

Introduction   7

Biographical Sketch   9

The Story Behind the Story   13

List of Characters   15

Summary and Analysis   17

Critical Views   59

   Charlotte Cook Hadella Discusses Political Influences
     on the Novel   59

   Charlotte Cook Hadella on the Novel's Experimental Form   63

   Peter Lisca on Symbols in *Of Mice and Men*   69

   Warren French on Arthurian Influence and Allegory   74

   Warren French on Steinbeck's Philosophies in
     *Of Mice and Men*   78

   John Seelye on Charges of Steinbeck's Sentimentalism   82

   Louis Owens Explores the Significance of George and
     Lennie's Dream   84

   Howard Levant Explains How the Novel's Form Shows
     Steinbeck's Skill   88

   Warren French Discusses Pessimism and Crooks   100

   John Timmerman on Locations and Frames in the Novel   102

   Lawrence William Jones on Why *Of Mice and Men*
     Is Not a Parable   107

   Marilyn Chandler McEntyre on Cain, Abel, and Innocence   109

   William Goldhurst on the Novel's Vision   115

Works by John Steinbeck   123

Annotated Bibliography   124

Contributors   126

Acknowledgments   129

Index   131

# Introduction

HAROLD BLOOM

The late Anthony Burgess, in a touching salute from one professional writer to another, commended *Of Mice and Men* as "a fine novella (or play with extended stage directions) which succeeds because it dares sentimentality." Rereading *Of Mice and Men*, I remain impressed by its economical intensity, which has authentic power, though the sentimentality sometimes seems to me excessive. The book has been called Darwinian and naturalistic; it does share in the kind of dramatic pathos featured also in the plays of Eugene O'Neill and the novels of Theodore Dreiser. Reality is harsh and ultimately scarcely to be borne; dreams and delusions alone allow men to keep going. George and Lennie share the hopeless dream of a little ranch of their own, where George could keep the well-meaning but disaster-prone Lennie out of trouble and sorrow. As several critics have noted, this is one of Steinbeck's recurrent dreams of a lost Eden, sadly illusory yet forever beckoning.

As in the works of O'Neill and of Dreiser, the anxiety that afflicts all of Steinbeck's male protagonists is a desperate solitude. Despite his frequent use of Biblical style, more marked in *The Grapes of Wrath* than in *Of Mice and Men*, Steinbeck was anything but a religious writer, by temperament and by belief. His heavy naturalism is very close to fatalism: Lennie is doomed by his nature, which craves affection, softness, the childlike, yet which is overwhelmingly violent and pragmatically brutal because of childish bafflement and defensiveness. What could anyone have done to save Lennie? Since George is truly responsible and caring and still fails to keep Lennie safe, it seems clear that even institutionalization could not have saved Steinbeck's most pathetic version of natural man. That returns the burden of Steinbeck's sad fable to Steinbeck himself: What has the author done for himself as a novelist by telling us this overdetermined story, and what do we gain as readers by attending to it? Though there are dramatic values in *Of Mice and Men*, they are inadequate compared to O'Neill at his best. There is an authentic dignity in the brotherhood of George and Lennie, but it too seems stunted compared to the massive humanity of the major figures in Dreiser's strongest narratives, *Sister Carrie* and *An American Tragedy*. Clearly there is something that endures in *Of Mice and Men* as in *The Grapes of Wrath*, though the novella lacks the social force of Steinbeck's major novel. Is it the stoic minimalism of George and Lennie and their fellow wandering ranch hands that somehow achieves a memorable image of human value?

Steinbeck resented Hemingway because he owed Hemingway too much, both in style and in the perception of the aesthetic dignity of natural men, at once unable to bear either society or solitude. The counterinfluence in *Of Mice and Men* seems to be the Faulkner of *The Sound and the Fury*, particularly in the representation of poor Lennie, who may have in him a trace of the benign idiot, Benjy. Any comparison of Faulkner and Steinbeck will tend to lessen Steinbeck, who is overmatched by Faulkner's mythic inventiveness and consistent strength of characterization. Yet there is a mythic quality to *Of Mice and Men*, a clear sense that Lennie and George ultimately represent something larger than either their selves or their relationship. They touch a permanence because their mutual care enhances both of them. That care cannot save Lennie, and it forces George to execute his friend to save him from the hideous violence of a mob. But the care survives Lennie's death; Slim's recognition of the dignity and the value of the care is the novel's final gesture, and is richly shared by the reader.

Biographical Sketch

John Steinbeck was born in Salinas, California, in 1902. Located near Monterey Bay, Salinas is still an agricultural hub in north-central California, near Sacramento. Though still viewed as a working area, it is also a tourist attraction, and is a far different place for its workers than when it was the very rural Salinas from 1910 through the 1930s. Studded with large ranches, farms, and orchards, Salinas (and neighboring Sacramento, Carmel, and Monterey) also attracted migrant workers and families who left the dustbowls of the Great Plains for work in California's growing agricultural economy. The influx of immigrants, along with the poor and displaced, created conflicts in the communities that Steinbeck mined in much of his work.

Steinbeck's father, also John, worked in Monterey County government most of his life, after an early failure as a businessman. The author's grandparents owned a large ranch in the area, and some of Steinbeck's first work experiences were as a hand on their ranch.

Steinbeck's mother, Olive, was a teacher, and is credited with fostering her son's love for literature. Steinbeck was not a particularly stellar student, but he did show promise as a writer. While he earned entrance into Stanford in 1919, and studied marine biology, he did so in a desultory way, frequently missing classes or semesters. To support himself during his time at Stanford, he worked as a farm laborer, or at the sugar plant, or as a fruit picker. These experiences put him in contact with drifters, migrant workers, and other dispossessed individuals, providing him many of the character resources he would later draw on. Even then, he knew his real aspiration was to be a writer, and so he relished his off-again, on-again approach to the university, negotiating his genuine interest in sea life and ecology with a more bohemian approach to living.

He stopped attending classes by 1926, and never earned a degree. However, he did gain a few things. One was advice from an English professor to use less stilted and inflated language, to keep his sentences direct and shorter, more to the point. The lesson stuck. He also learned the need for discipline as a writer.

When he left Stanford, Steinbeck headed to New York to earn a living as a journalist. However, he soon returned to Salinas, where he took odd jobs, including that of a watchman for a house in High Sierra. During that time, he wrote his first novel, the swashbuckling adventure *Cup of Gold*. The book did not do well. But its portrayal of the pirate Henry Morgan revealed Steinbeck's affinity for tales of morality and consequence (two of the young Steinbeck's favorite reads were Dostoevsky's *Crime and Punishment* and Mallory's *Le Morte d'Arthur*), even though his later work would reject determinism.

Through the early Thirties, he continued to write, publishing two other novels that disappeared quickly. He also married his first wife, Carol Hemmings, in 1930. They were quite poor, and lived in the Steinbeck family's vacation cottage in Pacific Grove, living on her modest income as a typist, a small stipend from Steinbeck's father, and loans. In 1934, however, Olive Steinbeck died, and within a few months, in 1935, Steinbeck's father died as well. With his books failures, his marriage failing due to what Carol perceived as neglect in favor of writing, and money scarce, Steinbeck was depressed and writing was difficult.

Finally, in 1935, *Tortilla Flat* hit pay dirt. With the novel a critical and commercial success, Steinbeck became famous. At the same time, he had developed a friendship with the biologist Ed Ricketts, whom he first met in 1930. Ricketts' ideas about the interdependence of living things influenced Steinbeck and many other artists and thinkers of the day. Ricketts and Steinbeck would be friends and collaborators until the biologist's accidental death in 1948. Ricketts' influence can be found in much of Steinbeck's work, but particularly in *Cannery Row* and *Sweet Thursday*.

Back in California after a trip to Mexico with Carol, Steinbeck found himself financially secure, among friends, and feeling creative, but he also found himself in a dying marriage and facing the realities of a writer's solitary life. The works published after *In Dubious Battle* (1936) cemented Steinbeck's reputation and are the most memorable contributions he made to American letters. In 1937, *Of Mice and Men* and *The Red Pony* made Steinbeck even more famous, and won him awards. *The Grapes of Wrath* appeared in 1939 and was made into a movie the following year. 1941 saw *The Sea of Cortez*, a naturalist work written from an expedition with Ricketts, and a novel resulting from his travels to Mexico, *The Forgotten Village*. After a few propagandist works (1942's *The Moon Is Down* and *Bombs Away*, both a result of Steinbeck's intense interest in and travels to report on World War II), he published *Cannery Row* in 1945, followed by *The Pearl* in 1947, and finally, *East of Eden* in 1952. While the list of titles is not exhaustive of his work during the period, the list includes what virtually everyone regards as the bulk of the author's finest work, the books which most clearly spell out his ideas, fascinations, and aesthetic.

All did not go smoothly during those years in which his reputation and fame rose. After the success of several novels and his divorce from Carol in 1942, Steinbeck married a singer, Gwyndolyn Conger, in 1943. With their union barely established, the writer left for Europe to cover World War II for the *New York Herald Tribune*. While the marriage did yield two sons, Thomas and John, Gwyndolyn's displeasure soon echoed that of Carol. She felt her husband neglected the marriage and the family for his writing. In 1948, he was again divorced.

As well, Steinbeck frequently retreated from his fame. Just after the success of *Of Mice and Men*, Steinbeck embarked for travel through Europe. In 1940, with the massive success of *The Grapes of Wrath*, and the subsequent ire of politicians and many in the agricultural industry, Steinbeck lit out once again, this time for Mexico. He returned from time to time to the Monterey Bay area, but seldom for long. By 1943, he was permanently settled in New York, with a summer home in Sag Harbor, and he made frequent trips to Europe.

By 1950, the writer was drinking heavily. His works were no longer popular, and many were out of print. He owed child support and alimony from his divorces, and he still owed money on many loans. He was nearly broke, living in seclusion in the cottage in Pacific Grove. He still wrote, but the task was as daunting as ever. Even so, *East of Eden* changed his financial circumstances by 1952, and Elia Kazan's movie of the same ensured that for the remainder of his years, Steinbeck would not worry much about finances.

At the same time, he met and married his third wife, Elaine Anderson. Elaine had worked in the New York theatre community, and so the couple lived out the author's remaining years in New York. Steinbeck's later years saw the author thinking increasingly about the state of the country, concerned as he was about the country's moral fiber, particularly the growing disparity between the rich and poor, the continued rise of consumerism, ongoing racial tensions, and the Vietnam War. He wrote moral novels during those years, including *Once There Was a War* and *Winter of Our Discontent*, as well as the nonfiction work *Travels with Charlie: In Search of America*. At the same time, fueled by his lifelong fascination with the tales of King Arthur and a year spent abroad in England studying *Le Morte d'Arthur*, he worked on his own version of the tales, published posthumously in 1976 as *The Acts of King Arthur and His Noble Knights*.

Having won the New York Drama Critics Circle Award in 1937, the Pulitzer Prize in 1940, the Nobel Prize in 1962, and the United States' Presidential Medal for Freedom in 1964, John Steinbeck died in 1968, at his home in New York. His ashes were returned to Salinas.

The Story Behind the Story

Steinbeck's earlier novels dealt with the many challenges facing American agricultural workers, as well as the challenges facing Mexican immigrants who arrived in California looking for jobs on farms or orchards. By the 1930s, automation had made such inroads into American farming that migrant workers, ranch hands, and the like were nearly extinct. The advent of massive combines used for harvesting crops reduced most farms' need for human labor. It was estimated that the combine did the work of more than 300 men, making farms need only a handful around for tasks in support of the machines. Thus, the realities of California at the time of the book's publication, 1937, meant that George and Lennie were two of a dying breed of itinerant worker.

Steinbeck's own experience as a farm hand provided some frame of reference for the book. While he did live with workers for a few years as a journalist, his own father had owned land in the Salinas Valley, so Steinbeck had been exposed to workers all his young life. At the same time, Steinbeck, like many writers of his time, including Thornton Wilder and F. Scott Fitzgerald, had a recurring fascination with the so-called American Dream—the idea that if one worked hard in America, the land of opportunity, one would earn a place in the growing and stable middle class. That dream was the acknowledged goal of many a migrant worker, and thus Steinbeck's early work often looked at what happened when the hopeful expectations of immigrants and the poor ran up against the realities of the working world.

Steinbeck wrote *Of Mice and Men* throughout 1935 and 1936, after having published four earlier novels which achieved neither critical nor financial success, as well as *In Dubious Battle*, which had attracted the author some attention. Some critics note that *In Dubious Battle* signaled the technical shift in Steinbeck's approach, laying the groundwork for the stylistic experiment Steinbeck only half-purposefully undertook in *Of Mice and Men*.

The book was the first of Steinbeck's self-termed "play-novelettes," works which functioned as novels but were written such that a theatrical company could perform them as plays using the novel as the text. Steinbeck started writing the story—a story he thought of as solid, independent of whatever narrative treatment he gave it—as an exercise. He was interested in writing for the stage, and so looked at the book as a way to work toward being able to write plays. He looked at each chapter as an act, the first paragraphs of which would set the scene and background, allowing dialogue, with minimal directions and other expository prose, to carry the narrative, action, and character.

The "exercise" grew into a short novel. Despite its success and Steinbeck's own thoughts about the merit of the actual story, John Timmerman noted, in 1986, that the author maintained a somewhat derisive view of the book long afterward, referring to it variously as "that Mice book" or "the little book." For all his dismissal of the book, however, he also wrote many years later in a letter, "This is at once the sadness, the greatness, and the triumph of our species."

The author's attitude might also have been borne of the conflicts he suffered while writing it. For one thing, he had to rewrite most of it after one of his dogs chewed up the original manuscript, and after already having once lost the manuscript for *The Red Pony*. As well, during the writing of the book, his father passed away, only months after his mother's death.

Still, the book was the most well-received novel the author had published to date, and the stage production won accolades from the theatre press and critics alike. The play version (which contains more than 80 percent of the lines from the novel) was short-listed for the Pulitzer, losing to Thornton Wilder's experimental classic *Our Town* in 1937. As well, *Of Mice and Men* was a Book of the Month Club selection before going to print.

Since its publication in 1937, *Of Mice and Men* has never gone out of print. Four movie versions have been produced, and the play is still routinely staged. Steinbeck's nearly dismissed little novel, *Of Mice and Men*, is now one of the most widely read and acclaimed American novels ever written.

# List of Characters

**George Milton** is small, sharp and shrewd, narrow-waisted and wary. He travels with and watches out for Lennie Smalls, a large simpleton and workhorse. George tries to keep Lennie from trouble, but Lennie can control neither his impulses nor his strength, and so the men flee from most towns to find labor somewhere else, to work toward a stake and live, as George promises Lennie many times, off the "fat'a the land."

**Lennie Smalls** is a gentle giant whose mental powers are very minimal. He is a child in a very large man's body. He cannot control his urges, particularly to touch and pet soft, pretty things, but he means no harm to anyone. He reveres and follows George, and is enamored with the dream of one day owning a little place, living off the fat of the land, and being able to "tend the rabbits."

**Curley** is the son of the man who owns the ranch where George and Lennie find work. Hot-headed and always willing to start a fight, he also has a wife who tires of his pugnacious character and inattentiveness toward her.

**Curley's wife** is described variously as a siren, a tramp, "jail bait," and worse. Her physical presence is cultivated and titillating, and she enjoys visiting the bunkhouse and talking to the men when her husband is not around. In nearly every description of her, something is mentioned to be red.

**Crooks, the Stable Buck** is a black stable hand, exiled to his own room in the barn. Though his back is permanently injured, he is very good at playing horseshoes. The game is the only time in which he interacts with the other workers.

**Candy** is an old swamper, too aged and feeble to do much else. He befriends George and Lennie after hearing of their hopes for a little place. He has cash saved to buy into the venture, and fears he will soon be let go, dismissed as easily as his own dog was taken out and shot by Carlson. George and Lennie's dream becomes his as well.

**Carlson** is a thick-set man whose brutish and direct manner contrasts with George's calculation and care and Slim's quiet confidence. He takes Candy's dog out to the yard and shoots it, assuring the old man he is doing both him and the dog a favor.

**Slim** is the skinner, the unspoken leader of the bunkhouse men. His quiet, faintly menacing, self-assured, and confiding manner—matched with his presence and what is described as his very able talent for his job—makes him the quintessential working authority figure.

## Summary and Analysis

*Of Mice and Men* is considered the most successful result of Steinbeck's formal innovation, the "play-novelette." John Timmerman notes that the idea for a play-novelette came out of Steinbeck's work in blocking his short novel *In Dubious Battle* for stage production in 1935. That work prepared him for theatrical thinking, and in February 1935, he wrote to his agent to say about the then-fledgling version of *Of Mice and Men*, "I'm doing a play now. I don't know what will come of it. If I can do it well enough it will be a good play. I mean the theme is swell."

He eventually decided to write a play, as Peter Lisca noted in 1958, "in the physical technique of a novel." He saw the play's structure to have advantages of brevity, of keeping a story close to its theme, and of providing a way to manage action and digression. The technique produced a novel that, with very few changes, could then be read and performed as a play. This is why, John Timmerman notes, more than 80 percent of the book went into the play, *Of Mice and Men*.

While told in six chapters, *Of Mice and Men* has as its overriding structure the five-act play. The first chapter introduces the two main characters and sketches the conflict that has led them to their present circumstances. The second chapter adds antagonism, in the form of temptation for Lennie and a threat to the two men. The third chapter aggravates the antagonism, seeing the first confrontation between Lennie and Curley. It also elevates the tension by having Carlson kill Candy's dog, a preview of the book's final scene. Chapter four refines Steinbeck's theme by casting the "second-class" individuals—the rejected (Crooks), the old and infirm (Candy), the mentally feeble (Lennie), and the vapid (Curley's wife)—into a circumstance where they each feel their status. It also allows for Curley's wife to make a connection of sorts with Lennie, unbothered by other men, particularly George. The fifth chapter has the climactic action of Lennie's accidentally killing Curley's wife. While separate from the fifth chapter,

chapter six functions essentially as the final scene of act (chapter) five, the scene wherein the tragedy comes to fruition, where George must bear the burden of killing Lennie, for what George thinks is his own good, and must then return to the world of men to live with the knowledge of his deeds.

Each chapter begins as an act in a play would, with narration functioning to set the scene, describe the characters, establish the tone, and then letting the characters enter to act and react.

## Chapter One

The chapter opens quietly. The first several paragraphs describe a pastoral setting—the deep of the Salinas River, willows and sycamores, the sandy bank. Most of the imagery is imbued with green, the first powerful instance of color in the book and a foreshadowing of the color work Steinbeck's prose will undertake at critical moments in the narrative. Into the scene come a number of animals, most notably rabbits.

In the second paragraph comes the presence of humans. A path has been "beaten hard" by boys coming to the river. A low sycamore limb comes down near to the river, and it too is worn, from men sitting on it.

Following dramatic convention, when the characters enter, the narrative describes them as would stage directions. They are clad in denim, "blanket rolls slung over their shoulders." George appears as "small and quick, dark of face, with restless eye and sharp, strong features.... Every part of him was defined." The edginess of that first description remains with him through the book. George is certainty, intellect, purpose. He is vigilant and watching.

Described as George's "opposite," Lennie is "a huge man, shapeless of face, with large, pale eyes, with wide sloping shoulders." He is sloping and dragging, shambling, indefinite, indeterminate, and guileless.

Even as they arrive, their behavior reveals basic differences between them. While George calmly enters the clearing and sees to his hat, with the singular gesture of running a finger along the band to clear the sweat, Lennie drops on all fours and begins "snorting into the water like a horse." His impulse for water, his thirst, overpowers any sense or control, and so George has to stop him, and his fatigue with Lennie is shown in the prose with modifiers like "hopelessly" and "morosely." Even as George sits and hugs his own legs, worried and considering what to do, Lennie sees the opportunity to imitate George, wanting both to play and to be like the man who takes care of him.

Through the dialogue between them, it becomes clear they have just escaped a bad situation, arriving in town earlier than they had hoped and farther from the farm than they would have wanted. George is not only fatigued from travel, but he has had it with Lennie. George's admonishment of Lennie makes it clear that the latest incident, in Weed, is part of a pattern of escalation, of worse and narrower scrapes out of which George must pull the two of them.

The novel focuses on the last episode of a dangerous life together, and the early scenes and ongoing exchanges imply the tumultuous past that has led George and Lennie to their current situation. But the book also begins a cycle in its opening chapter, setting in motion events that will escalate just as George and Lennie's risks and flights have.

As George lays into Lennie about his work card, he discovers Lennie is hiding something. George demands to see it and learns it is a dead mouse. Lennie insists, "I didn' kill it. Honest! I found it. I found it dead." The exchange reveals that Lennie had in the past actually killed small animals while they were in his possession, foreshadowing death later in the book. Lennie tells George he only wanted to hold it, to have something to pet, and George tells him he can't.

George moves on then, to strategize. He goes over the plan with Lennie, revealing just how much effort it takes to earn and keep work for the two of them and to keep Lennie in line—and how much it requires of George himself to make everything work. As George says, and says often during the novel:

God, you're a lot of trouble ... I could get along so easy and so nice if I didn't have you on my tail, I could live so easy and maybe have a girl.

Peter Lisca and subsequent critics have pointed out that George's lament masks a realization in George that he needs Lennie as much as Lennie needs him. George considers himself different from the men of the bunkhouse, the men working through farms in the West. George insists on his and Lennie's difference from other men, attributing his caring for Lennie to duty rather than something inherent and necessary in himself. As later scenes reveal, though, George has a strong moral sense and a powerful sense of purpose. Lennie gives him a more easily explained rationale to be that way, especially in the company of other men. As well, as Peter Lisca first noted, "George needs Lennie as a rationalization for his failure." With Lennie in tow, George can lament his state without having to face that he is not better or different than others.

The two prepare to stay in the sycamore grove near the river. George wants not to show up too early, so they prepare to build a fire and cook beans. George sends Lennie for firewood, and when Lennie returns, George discovers he has the dead mouse again, having retrieved it from where George threw it. As George yells at Lennie, the big man starts to cry, and at first, George rebukes him: "Blubberin' like a baby! Jesus Christ!" Before long, though, he puts a hand on Lennie to calm him, explains he took away the mouse because it was dead. He promises Lennie he can get another one, keep it for a little while. As he does, Lennie remembers a "lady" who used to give him mice, and George tells him it was his Aunt Clara, a woman George knew and for whom, now that she is dead, he feels compelled to protect Lennie. George explains to Lennie that Aunt Clara stopped giving Lennie mice because he always killed them.

Lennie hasn't gathered enough wood, so George sends him out again. Once the fire is lit, he cooks the beans. When they are nearly ready, Lennie announces, for the third time, that he wants his with ketchup. George snaps, delivering the full version of his lament about life with Lennie:

> God a'mighty, if I was alone I could live so easy. I could go get a job an' work, an' no trouble. No mess at all, and when the end of the month come I could take my fifty bucks and go into town and get whatever I want. Why, I could stay in a cat house all night. I could eat any place I want, hotel or any place, and order any damn thing I could think of. An' I could do all that every damn month. Get a gallon of whisky, or set in a pool room and play cards or shoot pool ... An' whatta I got ... I got you! You can't keep a job and you lose me ever' job I get. Jus' keep me shovin' all over the country all the time. An' that ain't the worst. You get in trouble. You do bad things and I got to get you out.... You crazy son-of-a-bitch. You keep me in hot water all the time.

At the end of the tirade, however, he sees Lennie's "anguished" face, and he looks away, "ashamedly." He regrets the outburst, but part of him also knows Lennie will forget most of it, which makes dealing with it possible, but makes him also feel worse. Lennie then says he doesn't want ketchup, tells George if there were ketchup, George could have it all. Lennie then resorts to a familiar recitation of his own, the promise to leave, to strike out on his own, to relieve George. As the text reveals, Lennie knows well enough that to say such things will get George to come around. George admits his meanness, says he will get Lennie a pup, first chance he gets, since pups won't be so easy to kill. But Lennie presses his advantage and gets George to tell the story, perhaps the most famous repeated passage of the book.

George lapses into storytelling mode, into what, for an actor, would be a monologue. Steinbeck writes that his voice "becomes deeper" and that the words repeat "rhythmically":

> "Guys like us, that work on ranches, are the loneliest guys in the world. They got no family. They don't belong

no place. They come to a ranch an' work up a stake and then they get inta town and blow their stake, and the first thing you know they're poundin' their tail on some other ranch. They ain't got nothing to look ahead to."

Lennie was delighted. "That's it—that's it. Now tell how it is with us."

George went on. "With us it ain't like that. We got a future. We got somebody to talk to that gives a damn about us. We don't have to sit in no bar room blowin' our jack jus' because we got no place else to go. If them other guys gets in jail they can rot for all anybody gives a damn. But not us."

Lennie broke in. *"But not us! An' why? Because.... because I got you to look after me, and you got me to look after you, and that's why."* He laughed delightedly. "Go on now, George!"

... "Someday we're gonna get the jack together and we're gonna have a little house and a couple acres an' a cow and some pigs and—"

*"An' live off the fatta the lan',"* Lennie shouted. "An' have *rabbits*. Go on, George! Tell about what we're gonna have in the garden and about the rabbits in the cages and about the rain in the winter and the stove, and how thick the cream is on the milk like you can hardly cut it. Tell about that, George."

George tells a little more after this, about vegetables and a little cook stove and the sound of rain on the roof, but the core of what Lennie remembers is the rabbits, the "fatta the lan'," and how George and Lennie look out for each other. Having placated Lennie, George moves on to business, to ensuring that the next day will go smoothly. He instructs Lennie not to talk at all, and is pleased to see that Lennie remembers.

His instruction continues, as he entreats Lennie to remember the place they are camped. It becomes clear that George did not stop there simply to rest before heading to the ranch. In fact, the next chapter makes clear that everyone at the ranch would have preferred they arrived earlier, the day they said they would. George risks it because he needs to prepare for the trouble he fully expects Lennie to get into. George feels confident Lennie will remember the spot; as Lennie himself points out, he has already remembered that he is not to say anything the following day when they arrive at the ranch.

As they settle in to sleep, George making the outrageous promise that one day Lennie will have millions of different-colored rabbits, Lennie once again ingratiates himself with George, reminding him that he could go away. As George quiets him, Steinbeck quiets the scene: the coals dim their red light, a coyote yammers, a slight breeze moves through. Nature has reasserted itself, showing the mix of threat and comfort surrounding and enveloping the two men.

The entire first chapter contrasts the relative safety and friendship of the two men when they are alone in nature implicitly with what the reader learns happens when they are in human society. In 1958, Peter Lisca wrote that "for ... Steinbeck heroes, coming to a cave or thicket by the river symbolizes a retreat from the world to a primeval innocence." Lisca also says, "Lennie twice mentions the possibility of hiding out in a cave, and George impresses on him that he must return to this thicket by the river when there is trouble."

Louis Owens and Charlotte Cook Hadella, to name but two critics, expanded on Lisca to note the presence of an Eden metaphor in the book, especially in the opening chapter. Owens cites Joseph Fontenrose, who said, "The central image is the earthly paradise ... It is a vision of Eden." Not only do George and Lennie *seek* an Eden, but they begin the novel's events in one, and return to the same place with new knowledge, corrupting it. Lennie, without knowledge of worldly workings, enjoys only the pleasures of nature and its creatures, has a simple understanding of comfort. Whenever the two men leave the "garden," or natural world, they run into trouble. But even the garden/thicket will not remain perfect. The more Lennie learns, the more he realizes, the less a shelter the natural world remains. Perhaps this provides the reason he talks of returning to a cave, a more removed sanctuary than the thicket he and George occupy. The snake present in the description of the Salinas River is no accident; it represents the encroaching knowledge and "evil" awaiting in the larger world.

But critics have also noticed and written extensively about the novel's concern with the Cain and Abel story. If one considers the simplest question posed by the biblical story— "Am I my brother's keeper?"—the overtones are obvious, as Owens points out. But the Cain and Abel story also concerns murder, guilt, and the burdensome knowledge of one's deeds in the world. At the end of Chapter One, George is already burdened with what Lennie's actions have cost the two of them, and of what he himself has to do to preserve them. He does not yet know of the burden he will have to carry by the story's end, though he may have apprehension about the greater weight to come.

## Chapter Two

Opening again on description, Steinbeck this time describes the bunkhouse, the setting in which all of the action in the next two chapters will occur. Much detail is lavished on the apple boxes holding very few personal belongings for each man, suggesting what little they have and how isolated they are. In one of the few moments of editorializing, however, Steinbeck notes that many apple boxes held "those Western magazines ranch men love to read and scoff at and secretly believe."

The early note of yearning is a reminder of one of Steinbeck's major themes, not only in *Of Mice and Men* but in much of what he wrote in the 1930s. As Peter Lisca first noted, fundamental longings are essential in Steinbeck, yearnings for peace, for some existence in or with nature, for the satisfaction of basic needs and the comfort of honest work. Steinbeck constructed and addressed, in his own words, the "earth longings of a Lennie who was not to represent insanity at all but the inarticulate and powerful yearning of all men." Lennie simply lacked the mental and emotional capacity to "scoff at" dreams and ideals in public while secretly believing and needing them. In that way, Lennie is more "pure" than the calculated George or the morally compromised men who work the ranches.

Hadella posits that what others have called the essential humanity of Lennie is actually animal. "Because Steinbeck uses animal imagery," she wrote in 1995, "Lennie is a symbol of humankind's animal nature." If it is reason, or the knowledge taken from the Tree of Life in Genesis, that ultimately separates man from other animals, then Lennie's animalistic behavior is also an innocent and morally superior behavior, and one ultimately tragic in a world that has lost its moral footing.

Steinbeck describes the dusty light of the bunkhouse, how flies moving in and out of the beam "shot like rushing stars." After that suggestive metaphor, George and Lennie follow an old man, Candy, into the bunkhouse. Candy notes that the boss was "sore as hell" that they were late, and then shows the two men to their bunks. George notes that one of the beds has a can of insecticide above it, and he starts demanding the old man explain why he and Lennie are getting dirty beds. Candy reassures George by pointing out the cleanliness (and, while he's at it, eccentricity) of the bunk's previous occupant. The passage partly reveals the strange habits of the men working the ranches, but Candy's very lack of more specific knowledge about the man reveals how, although all the men live under a single roof, each is essentially alone, in contrast to George and Lennie.

Solitude is further underscored by the next passage, in which Candy recalls the one time Crooks was allowed in the bunkhouse, where the welcome was quickly followed by insisting that he fight another man, Smitty. Candy recalls how Smitty had to remain on his knees, since Crooks was disabled, having earned the nickname after a horse kicked him in the back. Readers learn then both that Crooks is black and that he might not have much fondness for the men of the bunkhouse, understandably. Not only are the men of the bunkhouse separate from one another, there is a further level of separation between the men doing the work, and those who can't or who aren't welcome, Candy and Crooks. Candy's own distance becomes clear as he reveals that, while the men tended to go into Soledad and "raised hell," he himself no longer had the "poop" to do so.

The boss shows up then, and the narration tells the reader that "he wore high-heeled boots and spurs to prove he was not a laboring man." Like his son, Curley, he, too, is small. He tells George he's not happy the two of them are late, but sets to recording them in his book. As he asks for their names and what they can do, George gives him answers. As George describes to the boss what strength Lennie has, Lennie slips and says, "Strong as a bull." George shoots him a look, but the boss heard it and asks Lennie, "What can you do?" At that point, George speaks to the boss again, working to regain control of the moment. But the boss notices that Lennie doesn't answer, and says to George:

> "... Why don't you let him answer? What are you trying to put over?"
> George broke in loudly, "Oh! I ain't saying he's bright. He ain't. But I say he's a God damn good worker. He can put up a four hundred pound bale."
> The boss deliberately put the little book back in his pocket. He hooked his thumbs in his belt and squinted one eye nearly closed. "Say—what you sellin'?"
> "Huh?"
> "I said what stake you got in this guy? You takin' his pay away from him?"
> "No, 'course I ain't. Why ya think I'm sellin' him out?"
> "Well, I never seen one guy take so much trouble for another guy."

Despite George's assurances, the boss remains suspicious. His suspicion underscores the oddity of two men looking out for one another in the work world the boss understands. As the boss leaves, George turns to Lennie and upbraids him for talking, while Lennie asks George about the lies he told the boss—that he had been kicked in the head by a horse, and that the two of them were cousins. The exchange highlights the risks George takes to ensure he and Lennie can stay and work, and how he has to manage Lennie and his outbursts.

By revealing no family connection, the oddity of their arrangement, and the trouble it all causes George, Steinbeck reveals an essential part of George's character: that something in George himself also motivates him to take care of Lennie. One such thing motivating George is the dream he and Lennie share for the little place. He needs Lennie's money and Lennie's ability to work in order to make the place even a misty reality, much less a functional one.

The dream is, generally, important for Steinbeck. John H. Timmerman states, in *John Steinbeck's Fiction: The Aesthetics of the Road Taken*, "The idea that the dream itself can possess a person and must be ordered according to some social framework ... this tension provides a recurring framework for Steinbeck throughout his early work, perhaps dominant in *Of Mice and Men*." (Timmerman, 56) The social framework against which George and Lennie's dream is ordered is the reality of migrant farm workers. In an itinerant life, they desire stability. In a life of individual distance, they look to some communal existence. In a life of scarcity, they seek abundance. And in an existence of men looking out only for themselves, they seek the assurance that someone else looks out for them. Yet, everything in the society they occupy conspires, intentionally or not, to undermine their dream. Timmerman continues, "The theme of freedom and constraint ... reaches an apex in *Of Mice and Men*, where the individual dream is tragically destroyed by society."

As George finishes with Lennie, he notices Candy and bristles: "Say, what the hell you doin' listenin'?" The old swamper then enters the room, his very old dog with him. Steinbeck describes the dog's sorry state, and it's clear the dog is near the end of its life, like his owner. Shortly afterward, Curley enters the bunkhouse, looking for his "old man," the boss, and as he does, he spots George and Lennie.

Curley immediately sees Lennie's size, the vulnerable look about him, and stiffens. Steinbeck describes Curley's glance as "at once calculating and pugnacious." He figures Lennie for an easy mark, a fight in which he can topple a much larger man with little work. He is surprised, however, when George steps in to shield Lennie from the smaller man's prodding. George defuses the situation, but Curley leaves with a thinly-veiled threat to Lennie: "... nex' time you answer when you're spoke to."

When Curley leaves, George questions Candy: "what the hell's he got on his shoulder?" Candy explains that Curley is a fighter, "pretty handy," who "like a lot of little guys ... hates big guys. He's alla time picking scraps with big guys." George warns Candy that Curley had best not tangle with Lennie, effectively foreshadowing the confrontation to come between the two men. Candy goes on to tell George more about Curley, about his wife, and about the glove "fulla Vaseline" Curley wears to keep his hand "soft for his wife." George responds, "That's a dirty thing to tell around."

The exchange and judgment of Curley's wife is an early flash of the moral superiority Warren French describes as essential to understanding George's character. Not only does George harshly disapprove of both Curley and his wife, he also is not charmed by the woman as are the other men of the bunkhouse. French describes George as a ranch-hand Galahad, remarkably pure and noble in intent. But his nobility ultimately persists and matures with the price of having to kill something within, done through his killing of Lennie at the book's end.

George and Candy move off the subject of Curley and on to the work itself as Candy prepares to leave and ready wash basins for the men returning from the fields. He appeals to George for discretion regarding their conversation about Curley, and George grants it. As Curley leaves, George plays his solitaire hand, a recurring gesture of his, one loaded with overtones of isolation. As he does so, the flies coming through the light have changed from stars to sparks, suggesting more of a threat. Following the image of threat, George warns Lennie about Curley, accurately predicting that Lennie will have trouble with the short boss's son, and that an encounter endangered their dream of getting a place. George again moves to the ritual (and necessity) of repetition, reminding Lennie not to talk, of the thicket by the river and to go there if trouble breaks out, and to repeat it to himself so he remembers. Their conversation concludes to the cries of someone calling for the "stable-buck," before Curley's wife arrives in the doorframe.

The dominant color in her description is red—the red of threat, of the ominous sky, and of fire, as used by Steinbeck in the novel. George avoids looking at her, keeps his eyes away and his tone tight, but Lennie gazes at her and lets his eyes work over her body. She stands so "her body is thrown forward," and when Lennie looks her over, she "bridled a little." She considers her fingernails, claims she's looking for Curley. Her ruse is revealed then by Slim who, walking by, plays the game with her, calling her "good-lookin'," but also calls her bluff. When she says she is looking for Curley, Slim replies, "Well, you ain't tryin' very hard. I seen him goin' in your house." The line foretells the kind of sympathy Slim has for the people on the ranch. While he plays into Curley's wife's game and doesn't appear to judge her for it, he also doesn't let her think she's fooling him. It's an apt introduction for his entrance a few lines later.

But before Slim actually enters the bunkhouse, George warns Lennie about another inevitability, a problem with Curley's wife. Just as it is inevitable, to George, that Lennie will tangle with Curley, it is also inevitable that Curley's wife will cause some kind of trouble through Lennie. George calls her a "tramp," and Lennie says, "She's purty." George realizes that she is "purty" just as was the dress in Weed, or the fur of a puppy, or the back of a mouse. As the two continue to argue, Lennie announces he does not like the ranch, and George concurs. But he also brings up the need for the stake, a reminder of the dream, of their purpose.

The field hands arrive then, heard splashing in the basins. At the same time, Slim arrives. Slim is practically mythological in the description given him:

A tall man stood in the doorway. He held a crushed Stetson hat under his arm while he combed his long, black, damp hair straight back. Like the others he wore blue jeans and a short denim jacket. When he had finished combing his hair he moved into the room, and he moved with a majesty only achieved by royalty and master craftsmen. He was a jerkline skinner, the prince of the ranch, capable of driving ten, sixteen, even twenty mules with a single line to the leaders. He was capable of killing a fly on the wheeler's butt with a bull whip without touching the mule. There was a gravity in his manner and a quiet so profound that all talk stopped when he spoke. His authority was so great that his word was taken on any subject, be it politics or love. This was Slim, the jerkline skinner. His hatchet face was ageless. He might have been thirty-five or fifty. His ear heard more than was said to him, and his slow speech had overtones not of thought, but of understanding beyond thought. His hands, large and lean, were as delicate in their action as those of a temple dancer.

Slim's description recalls tall tales, American Western mythology, the stuff in the magazines that the men "secretly believed." He is a man of potential violence—"hatchet faced," with a "crushed" hat—and great calm and authority. He is the only one to look at George and Lenny for the first time "kindly." As George repeats his and Lennie's story again (as he had for the boss) to Slim, the reaction is very different from the boss's wariness. Slim's tone "invited confidence without demanding it." Rather than denigrate George and Lennie as odd, Slim tries to figure why more guys don't partner better to survive. He says, "I don't know why. Maybe ever'body in the whole damn world is scared of each other." Slim's authority makes the speculation close to fact, and close to a thematic claim of the novel.

George is immediately comfortable with Slim. Before they can talk much more, however, Slim's opposite arrives, Carlson. Carlson, of course, is "big-stomached," brash in his reactions and speech. Unlike Slim, he "stares" at George and Lennie. While he does say he is "glad" to meet them, he laughs a bit at

Lennie's size, a small joke that only Carlson laughs at. He immediately asks Slim whether or not the skinner's dog had yet given birth to her pups. Slim says she has, and informs Carlson (and the room) that he has already drowned four of them: "She couldn't feed that many."

The line is the first instance where death is posited as a solution for too much dependence. But immediately afterward, Carlson reveals he has been thinking about the sad shape of Candy's dog, how it "stinks like hell," how it "can't hardly walk," and how it "got no teeth, damn near blind, can't eat." Carlson feels Candy deserves a new dog, that a lame dog is worthless. The implied critique is that all lame and dependent creatures should be disposed of and replaced. The argument gains force and poignancy in subsequent chapters.

The dinner triangle rings then, and the men start to leave. George realizes Lennie has already fixated on the idea of Slim's pups. George assures Lennie, "I heard him, Lennie. I'll ask him." But before they can make their way to dinner, Curley steps back into the bunkhouse, this time looking for his wife. George is curt with him, even insulting, and when Curley leaves, George again admonishes Lennie about watching out for Curley, speculating he himself might be the one to tangle with him.

As the chapter ends, the last two images are the twin tensions of the book. The first is Candy's dog, gazing about, half-blind, unsure of where he is or what is happening. The other is Curley, young, petulant, vicious, bouncing into the bunkhouse, looking clearly and with purpose into the darkness—the innocent and the cruel, the helpless and the calculating.

## Chapter Three

The description begins with the sounds of a horseshoe game after dinner, the only real outdoor entertainment the men have, aside from heading into Soledad to the cat houses. George and Slim sit beneath a light in the otherwise dark bunkhouse, talking, and it is clear George has just asked Slim to let Lennie have one of the pups, and the skinner has agreed to it. As Slim admires Lennie's ability to work, George responds "proudly." Then, like so many others have done, Slim observes how odd it is that the two men "string along together." Unlike everyone else, however, Slim makes the observation with a "calm invitation to confidence." As George grows defensive, Slim calmly persists, and as he does so, calls Lennie a "cuckoo."

George responds with a version of the familiar litany he usually delivers to Lennie, about how he would be better off on his own. With Slim, however, George delivers it more as evidence that he is scarcely better off than Lennie, in some ways. He says, "He's dumb as hell, but he ain't crazy. An' I ain't so bright neither, or I wouldn't be buckin' barley for my fifty and found." He pauses after the usual speech, about having his own place, and as he does, Slim sits, like a confessor, waiting for him. He "neither encouraged nor discouraged him. He just sat back quiet and receptive." Then, in the silence of the bunkhouse and in the small cone of light, George explains the root of his and Lennie's traveling together. The reader learns of George's act of fealty to Lennie's aunt Clara, a woman he knew. George also reveals how he came to watch out for Lennie, rather than mock and deride him:

> "I used to have a hell of a lot of fun with 'im. Used to play jokes on 'im 'cause he was too dumb to take care of 'imself. But he was too dumb even to know he had a joke played on him. I had fun. Made me seem so God damn smart alongside of him. Why he'd do any damn thing I tol' him. If I tol' him to walk over a cliff, over he'd go. That wasn't so damn much fun after a while. He never got mad about it, neither. I've beat the hell outa him, and he coulda just bust every bone in my body jus' with his han's, but he never lifted a finger against me." George's voice was taking on the tone of confession. "Tell you what made me stop that. One day a bunch of guys was standin' around up the Sacramento River. I was feelin' pretty smart. I turns to Lennie and says, 'Jump in.' An' he jumps.

Couldn't swim a stroke. He damn near drowned before we could get him. An' he was so damn nice to me for pullin' him out. Clean forgot I told him to jump in. Well, I ain't done nothing like that no more."

"He's a nice fella," said Slim. "Guy don't need no sense to be a nice fella. Seems to me sometimes it jus' works the other way around. Take a real smart guy and he ain't hardly ever a nice fella."

Slim's comments in response indicate Steinbeck's sympathy for the ideas of primitivism, a sympathy noted by many critics, and virtually all of his detractors. Many of Steinbeck's salt-of-the-earth characters in other novels and stories have purity of heart similar to Lennie's. For this and other reasons, Steinbeck's reputation continues to suffer accusations of his being a sentimental novelist, or a political novelist too simplistic in his moral characterization of individuals. However, considering the end to which Lennie comes in the novel, and the ascendancy of George as the individual on whom the story really centers (the only person who undergoes a character change as a result of the plot), charges of sentimentality run into problems.

Immediately after the confession, George symbolically retreats into himself again, laying out his solitaire hand. He and Slim continue to talk, mostly about Lennie, and Slim is able to coax out of George what happened in Weed. The revelation is important on many levels. First, it reveals that George feels he has found someone whose morals are aligned with his own, and who therefore can be trusted. He can confide in Slim; he senses it. And, because the incident in Weed dealt with a pretty woman, and was one in an escalating series of scrapes, it foreshadows that what is to happen on the ranch will be worse and will likely also involve a woman. And the only woman present on the ranch is Curley's wife. At the conclusion of George's tale, Slim says, for the second time in the conversation, "He ain't mean," and then, "I can tell a mean guy a mile off."

At that point, Lennie enters the bunkhouse, furtively, and

George knows he has a pup with him. We see that Lennie still does not understand that he can't take soft and pretty things whenever he wants, and that he doesn't realize the pups still need their mother. George berates Lennie, and Lennie leaves to return the pup to the barn. By showing that Lennie still does not understand the consequences of his actions, Steinbeck establishes a frame of mind in Lennie necessary for the book's tragic end.

As Lennie leaves, Candy enters, his old dog in tow. Both show their infirmity, the dog struggling to follow and Candy complaining of a "gut ache." Carlson follows Candy in, and the only four men then in the bunkhouse are George, Slim, Carlson, and Candy. Carlson begins to complain about the stink of Candy's dog and as he does so, asks Candy why he doesn't shoot the dog. Candy is made uncomfortable by the suggestion, interpreting Carlson's impatience with the dog to be close to what might be the farm's impatience with him. Carlson persists, missing in his insensitivity how much the old man is bothered by the talk, saying "He ain't no good to himself ... This ol' dog jus' suffers hisself all the time." Then, thinking he is helping the man, Carlson offers to shoot the dog himself. "Then it won't be you that does it," he says.

Candy feels the pressure to act, and sits up. He protests, saying he has known the dog its entire life. His and the dog's circumstances parallel those of George and Lennie. The man watches out for the dog, admires his ability to work, and sees it as gentle and in need of protection, despite the nuisance the animal clearly is. In short, Candy sees a value in his dog that Carlson (and those like him) do not.

Adding to Candy's discomfort, Carlson then suggests that Candy could have one of Slim's pups, as if replacement were possible simply because Candy would have a new dog. His eyes trained on the dog, Slim says Candy could have the dog. Steinbeck does not clearly state what Slim is thinking regarding the old dog, but he has to "shake himself free for speech" to tell Candy that Carlson may be right about showing mercy to the dog by killing it. Slim might have been, a moment before, a sympathetic face for Candy, but as the swamper looks around the bunkhouse, he cannot find someone to help him resist what is beginning to look inevitable.

A laborer walks into the bunkhouse then, interrupting the momentum of the deliberations and buying Candy a moment. He shows Slim a letter in a magazine, written by a former hand from the ranch. Readers only know that the writer, one Bill Tenner, was "little" and drove a combine. The detail that complements the goings on thus far in the book is that he was "little"—just as are so many in the bunkhouse, in literal and figurative ways. The passage juxtaposes a "little guy" making a mark, so to speak, with a different kind of smaller entity facing the decision of its uselessness.

As the talk of the magazine letter goes on, "Carlson had refused to be drawn in." Carlson's focus is on being helpful, on doing what he thinks is right, blind to Candy's reaction and discomfort. Candy's agreement is only in speech; his physical presence and behavior indicate that he is very much opposed to Carlson's shooting his dog. His last-ditch effort is to point out that Carlson has no gun. But Carlson counters: he has a Luger. The Luger was the sidearm of German military officers, an association that would have resonated with readers in 1937, given the recent past of World War I and Hitler's developing urges for empire. Candy asks if maybe they could wait. Carlson pushes forward. Candy looks to Slim for some hope and finds none. When Candy finally acquiesces, he lies back on his bed, in a posture of resignation, and Carlson then gently leads the dog out of the bunkhouse.

As he does so, though, Slim tells him "You know what to do." Slim wants to make sure that if it must be done, that it be done right—that Carlson respect the corpse, and that he bury it. Slim tells him to take a shovel, and Carlson grasps the skinner's meaning. As Carlson leaves, George closes the door behind him while Slim tries to strike up conversation, trying to put noise in the room, to distract Candy. He mentions how his mule needs to have his hoof re-tarred, and as the room falls silent again, this time George talks about Lennie, probably enjoying a pup. When Slim tells Candy again that he can have any pup he wants, this time the old man doesn't answer. Seeing what Slim is trying to do, George suggests a little euchre, a card game. Despite the game, the noise level does not remain sufficient in the bunkhouse to cover the noise of Carlson's gunshot. When the shot comes, every head turns toward Candy, and the old man then turns in his bunk, curls in on himself, and stares at the wall.

The discomfort in the room is palpable, as is Candy's loss. Only Whit, the ranch hand playing cards with a distracted George, seems oblivious. Slim is silent, looking at Candy the whole time, and George is himself distracted by the complicated fate of Candy's dog. As Whit tries to keep the game going, Crooks appears. Notably, Slim is the only man to refer to Crooks by his name, or nickname; what he doesn't do is call him Stable Buck or refer to him as "the nigger." In addition to being the only one really watching Candy, he also does not let Crooks do the work he can do himself: tarring the mule's foot. Crooks offers, but Slim says he can do it himself. The result of these few actions is to cement an aspect of Slim's character, someone respectful and honorable in a place where, the men all seem to agree, one finds few kindnesses and little respect.

Slim leaves, and Whit turns the conversation to Curley's wife, and then on to the fun the men have each weekend, heading in to "Susy's place," a brothel. He describes it as friendly, with Susy always "crackin' jokes," and he invites George to go on the next trip, to which George noncommittally responds with "Might go in and look the joint over." Only as Whit keeps talking does George cease to be agreeable. After a discussion of the other brothel in town, the one to which the men do not go, George finally says, "Me an' Lennie's rollin' up a stake ... I might go in an' set and have a shot, but I ain't puttin' out no two and a half." The move from agreeable and conversational to emphasizing difference underscores both George's moral makeup as well as the circumstances separating him from the bunkhouse men. It is a form of reasserting his and Lennie's mantra about relying on one another.

As Whit rebuts—"A guy got to have some fun sometime"—

in walks his counterpart in insensitivity, Carlson. As well, Lennie enters, back from returning the pup to its mother. Lennie sits and tries to keep out of the way. Carlson sets to cleaning the Luger as Candy keeps his back to the room. Candy turns once at a noise, to regard the gun and nothing else, and then he turns back. At that point, Carlson asks if Curley has yet been into the bunkhouse. He hasn't, and Carlson explains to Whit that Curley was looking for his wife. When Curley does look in and notice that Slim is gone, the men tell him Slim is off tarring the foot of his mule. Curley, clearly suspicious, bangs out of the house.

The moment brings George back to further talk about the stake he and Lennie aim to raise. As Whit speculates over a possible tangle between Curley and the skinner and whether he should go out and see what happens, George insists he will stay out of it, concerned over his stake and staying focused. Whit and Carlson leave to see what will happen and George and Lennie set to talking. George, again, lays out his solitaire hand.

George presses Lennie to see if anything was actually happening in the barn between Slim and Curley's wife and, when he is satisfied that nothing happened, George sets to contemplating how men's behavior gets them in trouble. In contrast to the dismissal of cat houses he gave Whit, he now extols their virtues as a mechanism to keep men in control, to provide a place where "a guy can go in an' get drunk and get ever'thing outa his system all at once," as a remedy to the "jail baits" like Curley's frustrated wife. The statement reveals what George sees as *his* moral superiority to the other men. For them, as a solution to their otherwise troublesome behavior, cat houses are good things; for George, however, they are not worth jeopardizing the stake. That he makes this moral equation while playing solitaire—once again withdrawn into self-concern—underscores how George perceives himself as different, unique, alone. In a final thought, George recalls a mutual acquaintance of his and Lennie's, "in San Quentin right now on account of a tart." (George's attitude toward cat houses, Curley's wife, and women in general occasions some critics to cite *Of Mice and Men*, and this scene in particular, with other works as evidence of a strain of misogyny in Steinbeck's work. It is up to the reader to decide the merits of such claims.)

The situation leads Lennie to think again about their little place, about living off the "fatta the lan—an' rabbits." As George talks about a place he has seen that might be the perfect spot, Candy—who has lain silently on his bed—turns over to watch George go through the story of the little place again. George's voice warms, his solitaire hand stops, and the persuasive power of the recitation is at work again. It is the longest single recitation of the dream in the novel—lulling both George and Lennie into a near-trance. It is the apogee of their faith in the abstract. It also occurs roughly at the middle of the novel, and is stopped only when Lennie, carried away by a vision of the cats getting into his rabbit pen, bursts out with how he will "smash" the cats and "break their God damn necks." While the violent outburst quickly subsides to grumbling, it is a flash of anger and violence in Lennie that brings the story of the dream—and thus, symbolically, the dream itself—to a halt.

The next moment is another influence that will put an end to the dream. Many critics, starting with Lisca and French, point out that the dream is doomed not only by Lennie's violence, but by the presence of others and their subsequent claim on and facilitation of the dream's fruition. By making the dream actually become possible, the mythical lure of it goes away, and George is actually threatened by the change to his existence, at the prospect that the tribulation so critical to his identity will actually cease to be a problem.

After the recitation, in the glow of imagination, Candy startles both George and Lennie by asking, "You know where there's a place like that?" George is on guard then, asking why the old swamper would want to know. Candy quickly points out that he has money—over half of what they need—and the willingness to help. Candy knows his days of use on the ranch are numbered, and that he has nowhere to go. He sees how George and Lennie look out for one another, hears about the place, and wants to join with them, to make his own future a bit more secure.

At first, George bristles: "We was always gonna do it by ourselves." But as Candy persists, promising to will his share to the men, and seeing if it were possible to buy the place at the moment, George realizes his and Lennie's dire straits (they only have "ten bucks") and the promise shown in having Candy's money. But as he does the mental figuring, talking out loud, it dawns on him that they could possibly buy the land at the end of the month. He says, "I bet we could swing her for that." Suddenly, the dream is not merely a dream anymore. Of course, it is also different, involving the three of them, and involving care and work and making sure there is no misstep.

Every time George tells the story of the dream, Lennie insinuates himself at some point in a way to actually stop the story, to stop the rhapsody, to symbolically undo the dream. But as Candy and George think out loud the mechanisms it will take to make it all work, Lennie is silent for a while. Candy is animated not just by the promise but by the complications of knowing what Carlson did to his dog. The connections between the dog's infirmities and Carlson's declaration that the old animal was useless are not lost on a man whose own utility around the ranch is limited and whose own age is making more and more problems. Candy does not want a similar fate to befall him, and he sees that George and Lennie are, indeed, for all their claims, different from other men.

As George finally agrees to let Candy join in on the stake and swears him to secrecy, the old man says one last thing to George as voices approach. He says, "I ought to of shot that dog myself, George. I shouldn't have let no stranger shoot my dog."

For first-time readers of the novel, the line will seem poignant, but little more. However, given the end of the work, how George refuses to let Curley find and shoot Lennie and how George enlists Candy to help ensure he will be able to find and deal with Lennie himself, the line is hugely weighted. It foreshadows the end of the book and, presumably, stays with George to resurface later when George is considering what to do in the wake of Lennie's violence.

Men enter the bunkhouse—Slim, followed by Carlson,

Whit, and Curley. It is clear from their discussion that Curley has accused Slim of fooling around with his wife. However, Slim, being the unspoken leader of the men on the ranch, is not rattled and only irritated by Curley's bluster. With Slim handling Curley, the others become more brazen. Carlson openly mocks Curley, and even Candy joins in. As Curley looks to reassert power, his eyes land on Lennie, who, Steinbeck points out, is still "smiling with delight at the memory of the ranch."

Curley is on him in a second, demanding to know why he's smiling. Lennie tries to stand and back away, and before George can defend him, Curley attacks. Lennie is confused and does not fight back, looking to George for instruction. George tells Lennie to "Get him," but has to do so three times, so conditioned is Lennie *not* to act when George is near. When he does, though, Curley is immediately in trouble, as Lennie grabs his entire fist in mid-swing, stopping him, and then proceeds to crush Curley's hand.

The image is horrifying. Lennie is bloodied, stunned, and afraid, looking "in terror" as Curley flops and struggles to extricate himself from Lennie's grip. George has to slap Lennie and coax him to let go, facing as much difficulty in getting him to stop as he did in getting him to attack. In the moment, Lennie's focus and immobility are terrifying, signaling the problems that occur when his singular focus is paired with his incredible strength. It is the novel's first direct glimpse at Lennie's innocent capacity for harm as well as all the conflicting feelings such a display inspires. It foreshadows just what it is about Lennie that will land him and George in difficult spots as long as they are together.

When Lennie lets go, he cowers, insisting that George "tol' me to." Slim is the first to comfort Lennie, pointing out that the confrontation was not Lennie's fault. He then tells Curley:

> "You got your senses in hand enough to listen?" he asked. Curley nodded. "Well, then, listen" Slim went on. "I think you got your hand caught in a machine. If you don't tell nobody what happened, we ain't going to. But

you jus' tell an' try to get this guy canned and we'll tell ever'body, an' then will you get the laugh."

"I won't tell," said Curley. He avoided looking at Lennie.

Slim reasserts his leadership, protects Lennie, and gets Curley on his way to medical attention, all in one move. Slim's total control of the situation inspires trust in the men, and in particular it works on George. (George's trust of Slim becomes critical to understanding the final scene of the novel.) But when Slim says, "I hate to have you mad at me," to Lennie, George clarifies that Lennie was not angry, an important clarification both for Slim and for the reader, to show that Lennie is without malice. George explains that Lennie was scared. Before long, Lennie is back to himself, worried only whether he will still be able to tend the rabbits. Of course, George tells him that he will.

## Chapter Four

The setting of Chapter Four bears noting, as it is neither the bunkhouse nor the river. It is, perhaps, the most isolated part of the ranch, Crooks the "stable buck's" room. It is isolated both because the men chose to bar Crooks, who is black, from the bunkhouse, and because Crooks himself reciprocally bars others from his quarters. But Crooks, it becomes clear, is also lonely, and while he has to maintain his crotchety demeanor as a defense mechanism, he secretly appreciates company, however fleeting.

The chapter opens with a lengthy description of the environs, showing Crooks living in the harness room, not even deserving of a space entirely his own. The items of his trade are arrayed around him, and his only real personal items are medicines, mixed together in an apple box beside the horses' medicines. Slim's can of tar is there, as are other of Crooks' personal possessions—boots, a dictionary, a shotgun, spectacles. Steinbeck tells us in narration that Crooks had more things than the average man, signaling not only his need for things, due to disability, but that he was more "permanent" than the other men, with nowhere to go and no other options. Even Crooks himself is described lavishly, more so than any other character except for Slim and Curley's wife. The entire passage suggests a lavishness out of proportion to Crooks' importance to the story, implying Steinbeck had a wish to make a larger point regarding Crooks and the harness room.

It is worth noting that the only characters in this very separate and very different place on the ranch are, indeed, very separate and very different themselves: Lennie, Candy, Crooks, and Curley's wife. Each is somehow separated or cut off from the men who, that Saturday evening, are in town at the cat house. Each is somehow frail or enfeebled or frustrated, and each recognizes it in the others. The chapter dramatizes the arrival of each of them, as they arrive at the setting's most removed locale, Crooks' quarters.

Lennie is the first one to show up. Having come to the barn to visit the puppies, Lennie sees Crooks' light and decides to visit the man. Being without guile or prejudice, Lennie sees nothing wrong in his wanting to talk with Crooks. Crooks tries to explain the problem: "... you ain't wanted in my room ... 'cause I'm black." The explanation is lost on Lennie, who tells Crooks that George told him to stay out of trouble. Lennie saw Crooks' light, so figured he could "come in an' set." All Lennie wants is company—which, to some degree, is all Crooks wants as well, though he does not want to admit it, given how he has been treated by the men of the ranch.

Lennie tells Crooks he has come to see the pups, his pup, and Crooks gets gruff again, telling Lennie to go see the pup, if that's what he came to do. But as Lennie keeps talking, his "disarming" smile works on Crooks, "defeating" the other man's resolve. Lennie comes into the room, and as Crooks makes small talk about the men gone to the cat house, Lennie reveals that Candy is still in the bunkhouse, "figuring." When Lennie reveals that Candy is figuring "'bout the rabbits," Crooks dismisses it as crazy talk at first. But as Lennie continues, Crooks draws him out. Before long, Lennie has begun to tell Crooks about the dream he and George have.

Crooks, however, is more interested in the dynamic between George and Lennie. Crooks is more than just another guy marveling at the unusual bond the two have. Crooks has never had real companionship. He explains to Lennie, despite knowing Lennie will neither understand nor remember what he says:

> Crooks leaned forward over the edge of the bunk. "I ain't a Southern Negro," he said. "I was born right here in California. My old man had a chicken ranch, 'bout ten acres. The white kids come to play at our place, an' sometimes I went to play with them, and some of them was pretty nice. My ol' man didn't like that. I never knew till long later why he didn't like that. But I know now." He hesitated, and when he spoke again, his voice was softer. "There wasn't another colored family for miles around. And now there ain't a colored man on this ranch an' there's jus' one family in Soledad." He laughed. "If I say something, why it's just a nigger sayin' it."
>
> Lennie asked, "How long you think it'll be before them pups will be old enough to pet?"
>
> Crooks laughed again. "A guy can talk to you an' be sure you won't go blabbin'. Couple of weeks an' them pups'll be all right. George knows what he's about. Jus' talks, an' you don't understand nothing." He leaned forward excitedly. "This is just a nigger talkin', an' a busted-back nigger. So it don't mean nothing, see? You couldn't remember it anyways. I seen it over an' over—a guy talkin' to another guy and it don't make no difference if he don't hear or understand. The thing is, they're talkin', or they're settin' still not talkin'. It don't make no difference." His excitement had increased until he pounded his knee with his hand. "George can tell you screwy things, and it don't matter. It's just the talking. It's just bein' with another guy. That's all."

Crooks' monologue reveals a few things. First, Crooks acknowledges his own diminished role and presence in the fellowship of the dominant culture of the ranch, and in the dominant culture of the area in general. He's not white; therefore what he says is not taken seriously. In this way, Crooks has much in common with Lennie, Candy, and Curley's wife, each of whom is dismissed similarly due to perceptions that they are, respectively, too crazy, too old, and too much of a "tart," to use George's term.

But Crooks also goes on to articulate why such separation is harmful. He notes that companionship is important, that it is everything: "just bein' with another guy. That's all." He recognizes the fortunate circumstances that Lennie and George have. That Steinbeck chooses to have a marginalized character make the observation of companionship's importance signals recognition that the world of men that dominates the novel does not feel similarly. The world of the ranch hands is very individual and very lonely.

Crooks is also embittered. In a piece first published in 1994, Warren French noted that Crooks, one of Steinbeck's only important black characters, "articulated ... the pessimistic vision behind the tale ... in an attack on the proletarian novelist's vision of a worker's paradise." Thus, Crooks pauses at the end of his monologue, and when he speaks again, it is with the intent of upsetting Lennie. He begins to muse on the possibility that something might happen to George, that he might not return. As he does so, Lennie grows increasingly upset, refusing to believe that George would abandon him. When Crooks insinuates that something would happen, beyond George's control, to keep him from returning, and that Lennie would go to the "booby hatch," Lennie becomes at first terrified and then angry. Crooks' effort to dismantle the dream pushes Lennie toward rage. As he does so, though, Crooks realizes the danger he courts when Lennie stands and begins to approach him. Backpedaling, Crooks reassures Lennie, tells him George is all right, that he will be back.

The effect of his change in direction is to underscore his earlier claims about companionship. He points out to Lennie, "You got George. You *know* he's goin' to come back. S'pose you didn't have nobody. S'pose you couldn't go into the bunkhouse

and play rummy 'cause you was black. How'd you like that? ...
A guy goes nuts if he ain't got nobody." Lennie, however,
doesn't notice the change in Crooks' manner, in his message.
Still worried over George, Lennie remains agitated. Crooks
tries to reassure him, to show him that he has George and that
George will, indeed, return.

As Crooks lapses into a memory of his father's chicken ranch
and the bucolic days of his youth, the tone and specifics bring
Lennie back to the rabbits, and back to the story about the
dream that began the conversation. For all of his talk of
companionship and recognizing it in George and Lennie,
Crooks still doesn't buy that their dream will amount to much.
Crooks tells Lennie how many men he's seen over the years
with a dream, and how many times it came to naught. As he
talks, he hears a noise and thinks it's Slim, pointing out to
Lennie that Slim looks out for the team. It is clear that respect
for Slim comes from all quarters, including Crooks.

Slim is not the one in the barn; it is Candy, who has come
looking for Lennie. Candy hovers in the doorway, knowing the
unwritten rule not to enter Crooks' room. Candy addresses
Lennie, tells him how he was figuring about the rabbits.
Crooks, happy to have the company, invites Candy in, while
trying to be gruff about it. As Candy marvels over his first ever
entrance to Crooks' room, Crooks notes that only Slim had
ever been there.

Lennie remains fixed on Candy's talk about the rabbits, and
insists that Candy return to the subject. As Candy starts to
mention that he believes they can make some money with the
rabbits, Crooks interrupts and tells them their plan for land
will never fly. As they argue, Candy reveals that they already
have the money they need, and Crooks' tone changes. When
he realizes it might just happen, he is as seduced as the others
by the idea of a place. He touches his back, reminding readers
of his state, enfeebled by past injuries, good for little heavy
work, the kind most valued on the ranch. And like Candy, he
will only get older and more infirm. He tells Candy and Lennie
that he can work, can help, and in so stating effectively asks to
be part of the group.

Before either Lennie or Candy can respond, Curley's wife breaks in, asking them if they have seen her husband. She surprises them. None of the men heard her walk up, and none know how long she had stood in the doorway. As she looks them over, she notes, "They left all the weak ones here," underscoring the thematic substance of the chapter. She tells them she knows where the men, even Curley, went.

Crooks and Candy work to avoid looking at her, but Lennie is enthralled. She is amused by the variety of reaction, but mostly by the fact that none of them will talk to her. Her observations resonate with Crooks' earlier comments about companionship:

> "Funny thing," she said. "If I catch any one man, and he's alone, I get along fine with him. But just let two of the guys get together an' you won't talk. Jus' nothing but mad." She dropped her fingers and put her hands on her hips. "You're all scared of each other, that's what. Ever' one of you's scared the rest is goin' to get something on you."
>
> After a pause Crooks said, "Maybe you better go along to your own house now. We don't want no trouble."
>
> "Well, I ain't giving you no trouble. Think I don't like to talk to somebody ever' once in a while? Think I like to stick in that house alla time?"

Her observation about fear comes after Crooks essentially told Lennie he could talk to him because he knew nothing would come of it. There would be no remembrance, and thus no regret. Lennie would not have, as Curley's wife puts it, "something on" him. Her comments also underscore the isolation among men, borne of fear. But they are also disingenuous. It becomes very clear that the reason she seeks companionship is hatred of her husband.

She complains bitterly about Curley, about his pugnacious behavior and lack of attention. As she does, and she remembers the company in which she has found herself, she asks what happened to Curley's hand. The men do not do a very good job hiding that they know what happened, and she knows it. When they remain quiet, though, she erupts, castigates them as a "bunch of bindle stiffs—a nigger an' a dum-dum and a lousy ol' sheep," despising them for their resistance as well as the realization of her similarity to them in some ways.

Angered and flush with the recent realization that he might have a way off the ranch, Candy stands and proceeds to tell her off, his climactic point being that the three of them will have their land, their dream, and that they are better than bindle stiffs, that they are unique. She scoffs, just as every other character has done in the face of the dream. As she does, Candy regains control of himself and quietly reminds her that Curley might not like her in the barn, with the "bindle stiffs."

Curley's wife is about to leave when she notices the bruises on Lennie's face. Another moment later, she realizes Lennie is the one who broke Curley's hand. Upon the realization, she begins to flirt with him. She decides then, out of a powerful hatred for Curley, to seduce Lennie. Crooks and Candy realize what she is up to, and Crooks is the first to act. As he threatens her, however, Curley's wife begins the process of tearing down the fellowship that had briefly existed among them. She does so by bringing back into the room the various cultural separations that existed outside the harness room. First, she reminds Crooks, "You know what I can do to you if you open your trap? ... you keep your place then, Nigger." By reasserting the difference and the problem of his race, she reduces him "to nothing." Then, as Candy comes to his defense, she reminds him of his place on the ranch as well. "Nobody'd listen to you, and you know it." Lennie, too, is reduced, whimpering for George.

However, Candy also reminds Curley's wife of *her* standing. He announces that he hears the men returning, and says, "You better go home now ... If you go right now, we won't tell Curley you was here." Candy's threat works because Curley's wife also knows her word carries little weight, with her husband or anyone else. She was right in characterizing the group as the weak, in terms of how the rest of the ranch understands each of them, her included. Before she leaves, however, she sets up her next play, telling Lennie she was glad he "bust up Curley a little bit."

When she leaves, Crooks only partly comes out of his protective silence, enough to chase the other two out of the harness room as George appears. Candy, excited to see him, mentions the rabbits, and George scowls and reminds him that it's supposed to be a secret. As they leave, Crooks—once again firmly in his "place"—tells Candy he no longer wants to be part of the dream, to work on the place. In doing so, Crooks is the first to give up on the dream, and is thus the first sign foretelling its destruction. But his relinquishing it is bitter, because he has shown how much he wanted it to be a possibility. He has shown himself to the other men, and he has given up companionship and lied about his desires to do so. In a word, he is broken, both in his body and, once again, in spirit, just like Candy, and just like George soon will be.

## Chapter Five

Opening with a description of the barn, Steinbeck describes a lazy Sunday, "quiet and humming and warm." But the description itself carries some threat. The horses, for one, stamp and rattle at their mangers and halter chains. The sun slices into the barn, and there is the buzz of flies. Outside the barn, the men play horseshoes, oblivious to Lennie. As the description focuses on Lennie, trouble moves to the forefront—he is regarding a dead puppy, and he is worried.

The dead puppy causes Lennie to worry immediately about the rabbits. The mention of the dream right on the heels of Crooks' disavowal of it, and in the context of further dread, helps build tragic momentum. Just as the inevitable fact of Lennie's killing a puppy has come to pass, so too is it clear that an incident of greater consequence than the one in Weed is also bound to occur.

Lennie's actions with the pup foretell what his actions will be when he accidentally kills Curley's wife. He covers the pup in hay, to hide it, but then, worried and growing angry, he unburies the pup as he considers what it is George will do about the infraction. He grows angrier, then picks up the pup and hurls it back into the barn. Feeling bad, he goes after the pup after a moment and returns to stroking it, whispering how it was of little consequence, and so its death might not matter to George.

Given the previous chapter's exchange with Curley's wife, and her noting how inconsequential were the weak and infirm gathered in the harness room, Lennie's comments about the pup could as easily be applied to him. Given Lennie's fate at the end of the novel, his comments also resonate with Steinbeck's theme of the uncaring and impassive world in which the men's lives play out.

Several critics have noted that *Of Mice and Men* draws its power from Steinbeck's portrayal of a non-teleological world, or a world with no design or meaning or grand plan for the things that happen. To put it simply, things just happen. There is no reason, no rhyme, no cosmic consequence or order. In fact, one of the early titles for the novel was, simply, *Something that Happened*.

As Lennie sits in sorrow, Curley's wife creeps up. The narration tells the reader she is very deliberate, her face made up, "her sausage curls were all in place." Again, the only color noted is the red of her shoes. She is soundless until she is right near him. When he looks up, he hurriedly buries the puppy in the hay, terrified she should see it.

But she does. She asks him about it, and he reverts to the behavior George told him to use. He says to her. "George says I ain't to have nothing to do with you." He persists in trying to avoid her, despite her assurances that the men are all absorbed in the game, and that neither George nor Curley will notice anything.

When she notices the pup, she reassures Lennie that the animal's death is not a problem, that it may even be a benefit. Her assurances put him at ease, and she thus moves closer to him. As she does, Lennie again says how George thinks she will get men into trouble, and she gets angry. She then tells Lennie her story, revealing how trapped she feels in her current situation. According to her story, she could have "made somethin' of myself." Her dream—lofty as George and Lennie's, but in a different way—was to be on the stage, or "in pitchers" (the movies), given that men had come to town and offered her such possibilities. The man who made her the promise romanced her, probably got what he wanted, and then promised to write her. She never received the letter, which she unconvincingly claims is because her "ol' lady stole it." Just as George rationalizes how he is "trapped" with Lennie, Curley's wife rationalizes her failure as being the result of those conspiring to keep her from fame and fortune. The night she confronted her mother, she says, is the night she met Curley, whom she married soon afterward, just to get out from her mother's control. However, she tells Lennie, she doesn't like Curley and feels just as trapped with him as she did at home. She asserts again, finally, that she could have been someone, that a man said she "was a natural." At the claim, she "made a small grand gesture with her arm and hand to show that she could act. The fingers trailed after her leading wrist and her little finger stuck out grandly from the rest."

The effect of the gesture is to charm Lennie, who then sighs deeply. As if to remind them, then, of the risk, a cheer comes from outside. One of the men, Curley's wife observes, has had a ringer. Drawing the tension of the scene a little tighter, Steinbeck returns to description of the barn, in one of the book's rare descriptive interjections. The tension, for Curley's wife, is the wait to see if her calculated attempt at seduction is working.

For Lennie, though, it simply points him back to his perennial worry: the rabbits. He speculates aloud about hiding the dead pup to avoid trouble, and Curley's wife says, "Don't you think of nothing but rabbits?" He doesn't, really, and he then begins to go into the dream again, about how he and George will have a place. But Curley's wife doesn't care about that; she wants to know why he is focused on rabbits. His answer gives her the opportunity to circle back to her business at hand. When he says he likes to touch soft things, she tells how she does as well, "silk an' velvet." As they talk, she then describes how soft her hair is, and as she plays with her hair, she invites Lennie to touch it.

Lennie is entranced. He strokes the hair, and as she cautions him not to "muss" it, he strokes harder. She complains more, but he doesn't stop. When she tries to jerk away, Lennie closes his hand and holds fast to the hair. At that, she starts to scream at him.

Terrified of George and trouble and losing the rabbits, he pleads with her to be quiet, all the time forgetting to let go of her. He puts a hand over her mouth, then, to try to muffle her, and she struggles and screams. He keeps telling her George will be mad, but she struggles harder. Soon, frustrated and crying with fear and anger, Lennie shakes her, and "her body flopped like a fish." Soon, she stills, "for Lennie had broken her neck." And just as he did the puppy, when he realizes she is dead and that he had done a "bad thing," he covers her with hay. Her death resembles the deaths of the puppies, and recalls the incident in Weed; in its particulars and the way those particulars mirror so many of Lennie's missteps in the history to which readers have access, the death of Curley's wife seems, in retrospect, inevitable.

The events outside the barn reassert themselves, and Lennie grows aware of the clang of the horseshoes. Lennie's failure to understand the magnitude of his transgression is revealed when he sees the dead puppy lying next to the girl. Since he can easily get rid of the puppy, he tucks it in his coat, saying "I'll throw him away ... It's bad enough like it is." The lack of understanding portrayed in the moment allows Lennie to remain essentially an innocent to the reader. He remains sympathetic, despite the obvious threat he also represents.

But Steinbeck's sympathy also extends to Curley's wife. First, the "shepherd bitch," Slim's dog and the mother of the pups, smells the death on the body, and slinks away. Then, in the oft-cited description of her body as it lies in the barn after the killing, the narration makes even clearer the author's clear intent that readers see Curley's wife as a woman trapped in circumstances and whose behavior said more about her struggle than about character:

Curley's wife lay with a half-covering of yellow hay. And the meanness and plannings and the discontent and ache for attention were all gone from her face. She was very pretty and simple, and her face was sweet and young. Now her rouged cheeks and her reddened lips made her seem alive and sleeping very lightly. The curls, tiny little sausages, were spread on the hay behind her head, and her lips were parted.

As happens sometimes, a moment settled and hovered and remained for much more than a moment. And sound stopped and movement stopped for much, much more than a moment.

The paragraph begins with the aspects of her behavior that have gone, starting with the worst, and moving through the pain in her that no one saw, the "discontent and ache for attention," before finally focusing on the sweetness of her appearance. The narration helps her metamorphosis back into innocence. And when Steinbeck stops time for a moment, it is enough to reflect on the circumstances that simply *happened*, that brought her to an end out of proportion to her alleged transgressions, just as Lennie's end will seem both unjust and right, merciful and brutal.

Candy finds the girl, and trusting George just as Lennie does, gets George before he tells anyone else. Candy, like George and Lennie, has much to lose should the rest of the men discover the girl. George tells the old man that Lennie must have killed her, and George realizes then that Lennie will have fled. As George speculates what will be done to Lennie, Candy tells him that he is sure Curley will want to shoot him, as much because of the incident with the hand as for the killing itself. As George thinks on what to do, Candy speaks his greatest fear: "You an' me can go there an' live nice, can't we, George? Can't we?" When Candy drops his head, another part of the dream has died. Both men know the farm is now a very distant and unlikely possibility. It occasions one of George's two most important realizations in the book:

George said softly, "—I think I knowed from the very first. I think I knowed we'd never do her. He usta like to hear about it so much I got to thinking maybe we would."

"Then—it's all off?" Candy said sulkily.

George didn't answer his question. George said, "I'll work my month an' I'll take my fifty bucks an' I'll stay all night in some lousy cat house. Or I'll set in some pool room till ever'body goes home. An' then I'll come back an' work another month an' I'll have fifty bucks more."

The cat house bit is his standard bluster, but it is made the more bitter because now the only other option is not to watch Lennie, not to take care of someone else, but to become like Candy or Crooks, marginalized, irrelevant, alone in the world he knows and which he now has no hope of escaping. Just as Cain is damned to walk the earth doomed to his state, so, too, is George—even before he kills Lennie. Lennie's death is a foregone conclusion at this point, and George knows it. And George will suffer for it.

As George keeps talking, staring at Curley's wife, he repeats his familiar explanation of Lennie, how his actions came out of fear and not meanness. How his bad behavior never originated in bad feelings. As he does so, he realizes that he can't let the other men hurt Lennie. He tells Candy to give him a few minutes, to stall the others so that he, George, can get a head start. As George leaves, Candy takes up his part of the dream, and part of George's attitude: he curses Curley's wife as a tramp and says the entire situation is her fault. As he does so, he recites aloud some of the things he will now miss, his own version of the dream recitation George had so perfected for Lennie.

After a few minutes, the men, with George, enter the barn. Slim is the one who pronounces Curley's wife dead, his authority so complete that only his proclamation will make her death real to everyone. Curley's reaction is not sorrow first, but vengeance. He knows "who done it ... That big son-of-a-bitch done it." Carlson leaves with Curley, saying he'll get the Luger.

The same gun that shot Candy's dog will also be the instrument of Curley's skewed justice.

Particulars from the death of Candy's dog hang over the moment—the mob mentality, the rush to get it over with, the enthusiasm to "do the right thing" (though interpreted differently by George than the rest of the men), and a reiteration of Candy's own disgust and hopelessness. When Candy's dog was killed, the old man dealt with the idea of a similar fate being possible for him. Now that Lennie is going to die, he realizes the dream he had only recently taken as his own is doomed. Candy is twice disappointed.

As Carlson is off fetching his gun, George appeals to the only person who could make a difference: Slim. But even Slim, despite his compassion for George's and Lennie's predicaments, will not go against what seems so inevitable. He tells George that they will have to get Lennie. George asks if Slim could help ensure some mercy for Lennie:

> George stepped close. "Couldn' we maybe bring him in an' they lock him up? He's nuts, Slim. He never done this to be mean."
>
> Slim nodded. "We might," he said. "But Curley's gonna want to shoot 'im. Curley's still mad about his hand. An' suppose they lock him up an' strap him down and put him in a cage. That ain't no good, George."

The tide of inevitability is strong here, building momentum from the first moments of the book. From the first scene, where the history of Lennie's troubles first came to light, the book has moved inexorably toward a tragic end. Even the little sympathy available in this rough place cannot stand up to inevitability. The events have played out such that Lennie's death is the only possible outcome. Curley's personality has led to a confrontation with a man whose power and innocence both were incredible. Lennie could not have reacted any differently to his environment than Curley could have to his. Once again, noting that *Of Mice and Men* is Steinbeck's highest expression of his belief in a non-teleological world, the inevitability of the novel is underscored by its original title, *Something that Happened*, showing how little stock the author put in things having some reason for being. For all the pathos in the plight and death of Lennie, of all the weak people struggling against the brute forces of the ranch, the sum is simply something that happened. No meaning, no fate, no avoiding it.

Carlson returns and announces his Luger is gone, assuming that Lennie took it. At the same time, Curley announces that George will stay with them as they look for Lennie, using Crooks' shotgun instead of the Luger. When George tries to suggest maybe the gun was lost, Carlson says, "No, it's been took."—the party of men is unwilling to extend mercy. George tries to remind Curley that Lennie did not act out of malice, but Curley won't hear it. Slim notes that the widower may want to stay with his wife, but his taste is for vengeance rather than mourning.

As they leave, calling George to go with them so they "don't think you had nothin' to do with this," Candy lies down in the hay, his arm over his eyes, recalling the position he assumed last time there was a death on the ranch.

## Chapter Six

The final chapter is essentially a single scene, and it brings the story back to the little clearing by the Salinas. The imagery of the opening scene is back as well: the sycamores, the water snake, the shade and the mountains in the distance. Compared to the bedlam of the previous scene, the tone is much quieter, the scene more tranquil. A wind rushes in, a threat of storm, turning over leaves and rippling the pool, and the water snake is swiftly snagged and eaten by a heron. In the calm of the moment, a small death occurs, and then, before long, another snake returns, and as it does, calm again settles over the clearing. The point is clear: Lennie's death, however powerful it may be on an individual basis, will scarcely ripple the pond of the world, will scarcely matter moments after it occurs.

After the calm returns to the clearing, Lennie appears, creeping into the safe place he and George agreed upon only a week earlier. This time, instead of drinking deeply and sloppily, he barely touches his lips to the water's surface. He is attentive to his surroundings, knowing the trouble into which he has put himself. The world comes into high relief around him, with light climbing "out of the valley, and as it went, the tops of the mountains seemed to blaze with increasing brightness."

At that moment, Lennie begins a monologue, repeating ideas similar to what he has said all along in the novel: "George gonna give me hell ... I can go right off there an' find a cave ... an' never have no ketchup." He even appropriates the voice of his aunt Clara, chastising himself the way George would have done, using the same phrases George always used, including how George could have had a good time, "raised hell in a whore house ... coulda set in a pool room and played snooker." The litany brings all the warnings and the small, personal quality of the tragedy to the forefront, as if juxtaposing the deep, personal, and almost ritualistic end with the uncaring surroundings.

Then, as he lands on the ultimate expression of trouble and despair—"George ain't gonna let me tend no rabbits now"— Lennie hallucinates an enormous rabbit standing in front of him. It has his voice, and begins to castigate Lennie, calling him "crazy" and unfit to tend rabbits. The rabbit tells Lennie that George is sick of him, will beat him, threatening Lennie with some of his own deepest fears, the very fears Crooks approached in the scene in the harness room, in Chapter Four. As the rabbit's taunts become nearly unbearable and Lennie is crying for the rabbit to stop and yelling for George, George appears.

George sits next to Lennie, and it is clear he has somehow gotten ahead of the posse of men looking for Lennie. George's manner is stiff, worried, quiet. He has something to do, and it soon becomes clear what. George can hear the shouts of the men, and the light is softening around them as night comes on. The world has gone from bright to soft, harsh to insubstantial. Lennie is glad to see George, as revealed in his hope for George to now do what Lennie expects. He asks, "George ... Ain't you gonna give me hell?"

George then starts to, using familiar phrases, but this time with no anger in them. He says them "woodenly." When George can't keep going, Lennie then asks him to talk "'bout the other guys an' about us"—the story about how they take care of one another. The power of the scene comes from Lennie not realizing just to what degree George is about to spare him violence and horror, and from George going through the litany of the dream despite knowing that he is about to end it to save his friend from torment. Lennie is delighted as George goes through the familiar recitation, but George is quiet, halting, bothered. The wind moves through, and the shouts of men come closer.

George takes off his hat then, and tells Lennie to do the same, saying the air is nice. George hears crashing come closer, and as he scans the distance, he then asks Lennie to do the same, but so that he can imagine the little place. George says, "Look acrost the river, Lennie, an' I'll tell you so you can almost see it." George then takes the Luger out, and it is clear he has been preparing Lennie to be shot, to have him so entranced in the incantatory power of the dream that he will never see the gun, never know the moment of his impending death. George has to bear that burden.

George has to steel himself to do it. He tells Lennie about the cows and chickens, about the alfalfa, the whole time working his nerve to do what he knows he must.

When he gets to the rabbits, Lennie announces they will "live off the fatta the lan'," at which point George only says, "Yes." He does not go on. Lennie looks at him and George redirects his attention, again, to the horizon, to look away from George and the gun. Lennie then wants to know when they will do it, when they will get the farm, and before George says they will do it, he tells Lennie, almost as if confessing, "I ain't mad. I never been mad, an' I ain't now. That's a thing I want ya to know." A moment later, after saying they will get the farm "now," George raises his shaking hand, sets his face and steadies, and shoots Lennie at the base of his skull where it meets his spine. Lennie dies instantly. George throws the gun away from himself and, as he hears Slim shouting for him, he simply sits looking at the hand that pulled the trigger. Curley makes it into the clearing first, and sees that George has already shot Lennie, "right in the back of the head."

Slim is the only person who understands the gravity of what must have happened. He sits right next to George, very close, and says, "Never you mind ... a guy got to sometimes," words he could just as easily have used to comfort Candy. But they reveal, again, Slim's difference from the rest of the men. Carlson, representing something more brutish than Slim, instead asks George how he did it. George says, "I just did it." Carlson presses. George agrees to every detail Carlson comes up with, to weary to deal with making his own story, too stunned and sad to protest.

When George and Slim leave to get a drink, Slim continues to reassure George. But Carlson says, to Curley, "Now what the hell you suppose is eatin' them two guys?" The comment, offhand, insensitive, and stupid, signals how the world, like the river calming after a brief ripple, has closed back over a moment of suffering and pathos.

With Lennie dead, George is altered. He has both taken care of his friend and, in doing so, destroyed a part of his own identity. George is now no longer exceptional; he is now another man, on his own, looking out only for himself, with no one else looking out for him. When he leaves with Slim and walks up to the highway, he leaves the tranquil world of the clearing and crosses a barrier, the road, the great impersonalizing force of the twentieth century. The sense of futility echoes the poem from which Steinbeck took his title, underscoring the haplessness of efforts and hopes, the uncaring universe in which mice and men find themselves, and the viciousness of the world.

## CHARLOTTE COOK HADELLA DISCUSSES POLITICAL INFLUENCES ON THE NOVEL

Born in Salinas, California, just after the turn of the century, Steinbeck grew up in the midst of the struggle for fair labor practices particular to large-scale agriculture that depended on a migrant labor force for economic viability. In the late nineteenth century, agriculture had emerged as California's leading industry—an industry plagued from the beginning by labor problems. As commercial growers took over more and more territory, squeezing out family farmers, the demand for cheap, seasonal labor intensified, and community structures deteriorated. Though traditional agrarianists argued for a return to small farms as a solution to farm labor difficulties and civic instability, the rise of commercial farming and the economic success of agribusiness sufficiently silenced the idealistic notion of a good society shared by all citizens of a democracy.[2]

Steinbeck carefully observed farm labor difficulties, usually from the point of view of the laborer. As a young college student dropping in and out of classes at Stanford University in the early 1920s, Steinbeck worked on the Spreckels Sugar Ranches near Salinas. This experience brought the budding writer into direct contact with migrant workers, many of whom were foreign nationals: Japanese, Filipino, and Mexican. In fact, Mexicans had become the mainstay of the agricultural labor force in California by the mid-1920s as growers took advantage of the liberalized federal immigration policy toward Mexico and as the flow of illegal immigration from Mexico steadily increased (Daniel, 67). Added to this mix were a number of Americans of Anglo-Saxon stock whose ancestors had migrated westward from the eastern or midwestern regions of the United States in the nineteenth century; though they originally sought their fortunes in gold and land, many eventually hired on as wage earners for the lucky entrepreneurs who had beaten them to the American dream.

His experience with the multinational labor force of California agribusiness exposed Steinbeck to a kaleidoscope of dialects, customs, and characters, all of which became material for his fiction. One of his earliest published stories, "Fingers of Cloud" (1924), takes place in the bunkhouse of a Filipino work gang. *Tortilla Flat* (1935), his first commercial success, details the lives of the *paisanos*, people of Spanish-Mexican descent who lived in the hills above Monterey. Juan Chicoy, a Mexican Indian, is the central character in *The Wayward Bus* (1947). Given the multiracial configuration of the California labor force in the early decades of the twentieth century, we may conclude that in *Of Mice and Men*, where the laborers are white Americans, Steinbeck did not intend to draw an accurate sociohistorical picture. Still, the subsistence-level economy, the tensions between workers and owners, and the social marginality of the migrant workers in the novella ring true to the historical details of the actual setting.

Furthermore, by focusing in *Of Mice and Men* on the dream of owning land, Steinbeck was appealing to a basic desire of average citizens as well as the dispossessed masses, regardless of their race or homeland. Steinbeck biographer Jackson Benson notes that while Steinbeck and his wife Carol were living in Mexico City for several months in 1935, the author was deeply moved by the struggles of the landless poor.[3] This experience, combined with his firsthand observations of the miserable lives of migrant laborers, began to take shape in Steinbeck's imagination as an experimental novel, written like a play, that would dramatize the struggles of working people who were striving to become independent landowners.

The Great Depression, of course, intensified labor tensions in the farming industry in California. In the early 1930s, agricultural wages dropped to all-time lows and workers found it difficult to provide food, shelter, and clothing for themselves and their dependents (Benson, 293). Even before the Communist party appeared on the scene, California workers had begun to strike against the unfair practices of growers. In 1932, the Cannery and Agricultural Workers' Industrial Union was organized by the Communist party, and the frequency and intensity of farm labor strikes in the valley increased. It was difficult for anyone living in California in the early 1930s not to be acutely aware of farm labor issues: strikes erupted in the Imperial Valley, the San Joaquin Valley, Watsonville, Salinas, and the Santa Clara Valley. Young people who were helping to organize the strikes and ministering to the needs of migrant families were dropping by the Steinbecks' cottage in Pacific Grove on a regular basis. Also during this period, Steinbeck became interested in writing a biographical piece about the labor organizers; through a friend and organizer, Francis Whitaker, Steinbeck was able to meet people associated with leftist activities and sympathetic to the plight of the workers (Benson, 293–97). As Louis Owens points out,

> [t]hough he never wrote the biographical story he had in mind, this meeting began a process of education for Steinbeck that would culminate in the short stories entitled "The Vigilante" and "The Raid," as well as Steinbeck's greatest novels, *In Dubious Battle*, *Of Mice and Men*, and *The Grapes of Wrath*. While, contrary to widespread opinion, Steinbeck was never sympathetic to communism, the author's sympathies would from this time forward lie more and more with the oppressed migrant laborer, and his lifelong loathing of middle-class materialism would evolve into a powerful resentment of corporate agriculture in California.[4]

Furthermore, the characters of those great works of the 1930s were knocking on Steinbeck's door, so to speak, without even being invited. In writing *In Dubious Battle*, Steinbeck took note of the events unfolding before him to dramatize what he considered to be "the symbol of man's eternal, bitter warfare with himself" (Benson, 304). He was interested in depicting the dynamics of a group-man, a phalanx theory that would explain mob psychology and blind commitment to a cause in scientific terms. Thus the work took on a documentary tone.

Having succeeded in portraying a large-scale battle between workers and growers in *In Dubious Battle*, Steinbeck turned his attention to the more private struggle of two migrant workers longing to escape from a cycle of oppression by buying a small farm of their own. By 1936, the year Steinbeck was writing *Of Mice and Men*, the technological revolution in agribusiness was threatening what little job security itinerant workers had. Anne Loftis reports that mechanical combines enabling 5 men to do the work of 350 men were responsible for half the nation's grain harvest in 1938.[5] Cletus E. Daniel, in *Bitter Harvest: A History of California Farmworkers, 1870–1941*, writes that "[b]y the twentieth century, employment in California's large-scale agriculture had come to mean irregular work, constant movement, low wages, squalid working and living conditions, social isolation, emotional deprivation, and individual powerlessness so profound as to make occupational advancement a virtual impossibility." He goes on to stress that "whatever the differences of race, national origin, language, and psychology that existed among farmworkers in California from 1870 to 1930, working for wages in industrialized agriculture normally conferred membership in an unhappy fraternity whose cohering force was a kinship of powerlessness" (Daniel, 64).

In *Of Mice and Men*, Steinbeck features just such an "unhappy fraternity": barley buckers, a bunkhouse hand, a mule skinner, a stable buck, and a lonely woman. These characters are thrust into conflict with the ranch owner, his son, and a social structure that views them more as expendable commodities than as worthwhile human beings. They are challenged to discover and to maintain their humanity in the face of overwhelmingly dehumanizing forces. In this sense, their story is not just an American drama that takes place in a particular region of the country at a particular time in history; it is a human drama for all places and all times.

### Notes

2. Cletus E. Daniel, *Bitter Harvest: A History of California Farmworkers, 1870–1941* (Berkeley: University of California Press, 1982), 62–64; hereafter cited in text.

3. Jackson Benson, *The True Adventures of John Steinbeck, Writer* (1984; New York: Penguin Books, 1990), 326; hereafter cited in text.

4. Louis Owens, *The Grapes of Wrath: Trouble in the Promised Land* (Boston: Twayne Publishers, 1989), 3.

5. Anne Loftis, "A Historical Introduction to *Of Mice and Men*," in *The Short Novels of John Steinbeck*, ed. Jackson Benson (Durham, N.C.: Duke University Press, 1990), 39.

## CHARLOTTE COOK HADELLA ON THE NOVEL'S EXPERIMENTAL FORM

In the earliest stages of the writing experiment that would develop into *Of Mice and Men*, Steinbeck compared the thrill of literary experimentation to the "kind of excitement like that you get near a dynamo from breathing pure oxygen." He explained: "This work is going quickly and should get done quickly. I'm using a new set of techniques as far as I know but I am so ill read that it may have been done. Not that that matters at all, except that the unexplored in method makes the job at once more difficult because I can't tell what it will get over and more pleasant because it requires more care. I'm not interested in method as such but I am interested in having a vehicle exactly adequate to the theme" (*LL*, 124).

The vehicle Steinbeck crafted for *Of Mice and Men* was a form he called a play-novelette, a novel that could be read as such but could also be performed on stage by working directly from the text. Each section of the book is a clearly focused episode in which Steinbeck evokes the natural elements of sunlight, shade, and darkness to convey a sense of stage lighting and the opening and closing of scenes. Just as in his prize-winning short story "The Murder," each of the six chapters or sections of the novella begins with the physical details of the scene as the author sets the stage for the dramatic action that will follow.[6]

In the first paragraph of the book, our attention is drawn to the sunlight on the river; the water slips over the sand before reaching the pool in the grove where we will eventually meet George and Lennie. Once Steinbeck has shown us the valley in full light, he narrows the perspective to focus on the grove:

"The shade climbed up the hills toward the top.... And then from the direction of the state highway came the sound of footsteps on crisp sycamore leaves ... and then two men emerged from the path and came into the opening by the green pool."[7] In this excerpt, the clear, descriptive prose, though perfectly suited to the events of the narrative, can also be read as stage directions. The entire first scene takes place in the grove, with most of the action centered around the campfire. The episode closes as "the red light dimmed on the coals." With the fading light, we are given details of sound effects: "Up the hill from the river a coyote yammered, and a dog answered from the other side of the stream. The sycamore leaves whispered in a little night breeze" (*OMM*, 16).

Part 2 opens with physical details of setting so specific that a set designer could recreate the scene on stage with no further instructions; the prop crew would need no imagination whatsoever to furnish the room. Steinbeck mentions the shape of the bunkhouse, the number of square windows, the woodstove, the square table with boxes for chairs, the wooden latch on the door. There are eight bunks, "five of them made up with blankets and the other three showing their burlap ticking. Over each bunk there was nailed an apple box with the opening forward so that it made two shelves for the personal belongings of the occupant of the bunk" (*OMM*, 17). Even the items on the shelves are mentioned. The position of the morning sun, which "threw a bright dust-laden bar through one of the side windows" (*OMM*, 17–18), signals the rising curtain.

All of part 2 takes place in this room where entrances and exits are announced, and new characters are introduced by their physical appearances, just as George and Lennie had been described in the opening scene. The action begins with the raising of the wooden latch on the bunkhouse door and the entrance of Candy, George, and Lennie. As in part 1, the stage is set and then the principal characters enter. The tension of the story line increases throughout the scene each time the wooden latch is raised or some new character steps into the doorway. The ranch boss comes in, questions George and

Lennie, complains about their tardiness, and leaves. He is soon followed by his son Curley, who does the same. Sensing trouble, George reminds Lennie to hide in the grove if anything bad happens. Lennie has just finished rehearsing his directions when Curley's wife enters, literally casting a shadow on a thematically darkening scene. Steinbeck writes: "Both men glanced up, for the rectangle of sunshine in the doorway was cut off. A girl was standing there looking in" (*OMM*, 31). Steinbeck describes the woman, her attire, and the details of her makeup as she stands there, framed by the doorway, the sunlight coming into the room from behind her.

Walking into the light behind Curley's wife is Slim; she speaks to him and leaves, but his entrance is delayed until after George's warning to Lennie to stay away from the woman. Just as the negative energy of the situation seems to have reached a breaking point, Slim enters, freshly washed up for dinner, bringing with him an air of sanity and fairness. Again, the character description reads like stage directions:

> A tall man stood in the doorway. He held a crushed Stetson hat under his arm while he combed his long black, damp hair straight back. Like the others he wore blue jeans and a short denim jacket. When he had finished combing his hair he moved into the room, and he moved with a majesty only achieved by royalty and master craftsmen. He was a jerkline skinner, the prince of the ranch.... His authority was so great that his word was taken on any subject, be it politics or love. (*OMM*, 33)

Slim's presence breaks the tension that George created in his ominous words to Lennie. By drawing George into a conversation about work and fellowship, Slim gives George an opportunity to compliment Lennie's strength. Approving of the rare partnership between his two new workers, Slim, whom Steinbeck has introduced as a benevolent authority, sanctions the union between George and Lennie.

Carlson, another barley bucker, enters next and brings up the subject of Slim's dog, who has just had a litter of puppies.

Lennie becomes excited on hearing about the puppies, but the mood darkens again as Carlson details his plan for getting rid of Candy's old dog. George and Lennie head for the doorway to exit the bunkhouse, but just as they reach it Curley bounces in, looking for his wife. This chance encounter prefigures the serious encounter between Lennie, George, and Curley at the end of part 3. The scene closes with everyone leaving the bunkhouse, where "the sunshine lay in a thin line under the window" (*OMM*, 37). Candy's old dog, whose death sentence has already been pronounced by Carlson, limps into the room and drops to the floor. Steinbeck juxtaposes the dog's lethargy and Curley's restlessness by giving us one more glimpse of Curley, who "popped into the doorway again and stood looking at the room" (*OMM*, 37).

By the end of part 2, Steinbeck has introduced all of the characters and major conflicts of the story. Part 3 begins with stage and lighting directions: "Although there was evening brightness showing through the windows of the bunkhouse, inside it was dusk" (*OMM*, 38). Enter Slim and George. Using dialogue as exposition, Steinbeck economically fills in the narrative gaps between scenes while continuing to advance the plot. As Slim and George converse, we learn that Slim has given Lennie one of his puppies—a simple gesture that has multiple ramifications in terms of plot and theme development: George's gratitude and friendship toward Slim, further demonstration of Lennie's lack of control, more pressure on Candy to give up his old dog. The discussion between George and Slim about Lennie and the trouble he got into in Weed sheds light on the past and foreshadows the future. As the two men talk, periodically the narrative eye monitors the progress of time from early evening to darkness by noting the intensity of light coming through the windows of the bunkhouse. Candy enters when it is almost dark outside. Then, "the thick-bodied Carlson came in out of the darkening yard. He walked to the other end of the bunkhouse and turned on the second shaded light" (*OMM*, 44).

But the artificial lights of the room cannot expel the dark mood that has entered with Candy and Carlson. While

George, Slim, and Whit, another barley bucker, sit by silently, Carlson coerces Candy into letting him take the old dog out to shoot him. After the sound of the pistol breaks the tension, the scene is busy with numerous exits and entrances, punctuated by the pivotal conversation between George, Lennie, and Candy, in which the old man offers his life savings to George for a partnership in the farm George and Lennie plan to buy. For a moment, the dream of escaping the migrant worker's life seems to be within the realm of reality. The hopeful mood is quickly cut short, however, when Curley enters the bunkhouse. Thinking that Lennie is laughing at him, Curley attacks Lennie, and Lennie crushes his hand at George's command. The trouble George has been anticipating is just beginning, and there is no neat "curtain closing" on this scene. Slim makes Curley promise not tell his father what has happened, and then Curley is taken off to the hospital. George and Lennie are left alone in the room, and the scene ends.

Part 4 begins with a close-up of the room in the barn occupied by Crooks, the black stable hand, which is described in the same meticulous manner as the bunkhouse had been. Crooks's interlude with Lennie, though it seems to provide a lull in the physical action of the plot, develops Lennie's character further and reinforces the theme of the illusory land dream. With the introduction of Curley's wife into the scene, and the emphasis upon her interest in Lennie as the person who injured Curley's hand, Steinbeck sets the stage for the dramatic conclusion of the story. Part 5, the last episode of the story to take place on the ranch, is also set in the barn and opens with Lennie's lament over his dead puppy. Alone in the barn, he talks to himself, expressing his fear that George will be angry. He tries to decide if his accidental killing of the puppy should be considered a bad thing, meaning he should go hide in the grove by the pool. This is the first time Lennie has the "stage" to himself, and Steinbeck uses this moment to illustrate how truly dangerous Lennie is: he possesses tremendous physical strength over which he has no control, and he depends entirely on George to think for him.

Lennie's conversation with his dead puppy resembles a tragic hero's soliloquy in which he reveals to the audience his mind, his heart, and the motives for his actions. Lennie, however, instead of being a tragic hero, is simply a tragedy of nature, for we can clearly see he has no control over his mind, his heart, or his actions. Curley's wife, who meets her death at Lennie's hands, acts as a character foil for Lennie in this scene. Her gender appears to be a tragedy of nature as well: because she is a woman in a man's world, she has little or no control over her life; and because she has no understanding whatsoever of Lennie's power and lack of control, she loses her life in an instant. Instinctively, before fleeing for the sycamore grove by the river, Lennie covers the woman's dead body with hay, just as he had covered the dead puppy. Moments later, she is discovered, and the lynch mob is off in pursuit of Lennie.

The final episode brings us to the same setting, even the same time of day, as the opening scene. In the quiet grove where George and Lennie first entered the story, Steinbeck brings them together again for the last time. The day is ending; shortly before George shoots Lennie, Steinbeck returns to the light/shadow motif of the first three sections of the novella. He writes: "Only the topmost ridges were in the sun now. The shadow in the valley was blue and soft" (*OMM*, 103). This description typifies the narrative passages throughout *Of Mice and Men*.

Rarely does the narrative voice break from this descriptive mode. With his decision to write a novel that could be performed as a play, Steinbeck imposed rigid restrictions on the narrative discourse and thrust all of the responsibility for exposition and plot advancement onto the dialogue and action of the characters. Thus the reader hears and sees the story unfold. Significant actions of the story—Lennie's crushing Curley's hand and his accidental killing of the puppy and of Curley's wife—fall into place alongside the seemingly insignificant details of everyday ranch life. These various misfortunes have a cumulative effect; they add up, and finally the pace of the narrative slows at the most intense moment, when George shoots Lennie by the river. The effectiveness of this dramatic technique accounts in part for the enduring success of *Of Mice and Men*. In carrying out his literary experiment, Steinbeck was able to capture some of his own excitement in the pages of this popular American classic.

## Notes

6. "The Murder" first appeared in *O. Henry Prize Stories* in 1934; it was anthologized in *The Long Valley* in 1938.

7. John Steinbeck, *Of Mice and Men/Cannery Row* (New York: Viking Penguin, 1986), 2; hereafter cited in text as *OMM*.

## PETER LISCA ON SYMBOLS IN *OF MICE AND MEN*

In *Of Mice and Men* the protagonists are projected against a very thin background and must suggest or create this larger pattern through their own particularity. To achieve this, Steinbeck makes use of language, action, and symbol as recurring motifs. All three of these motifs are presented in the opening scene, are contrapuntally developed through the story, and come together again at the end.

The first symbol in the novel, and the primary one, is the little spot by the river where the story begins and ends. The book opens with a description of this place by the river, and we first see George and Lennie as they enter this place from the highway to an outside world. It is significant that they prefer spending the night here rather than going on to the bunkhouse at the ranch.

Steinbeck's novels and stories often contain groves, willow thickets by a river, and caves which figure prominently in the action. There are, for example, the grove in *To a God Unknown*, the place by the river in the Junius Maltby story, the two caves and a willow thicket in *The Grapes of Wrath*, the cave under the bridge in *In Dubious Battle*, the caves in *The Wayward Bus*, and the thicket and cave in *The Pearl*. For George and Lennie, as for other Steinbeck heroes, coming to a cave or thicket by the river symbolizes a retreat from the world to a primeval innocence. Sometimes as in *The Grapes of Wrath*, this retreat has explicit overtones of a return to the womb and rebirth. In the opening scene of *Of Mice and Men* Lennie twice mentions the possibility of hiding out in a cave, and George impresses on him that he must return to this thicket by the river when there is trouble.

While the cave or the river thicket is a "safe place," it is physically impossible to remain there, and this symbol of primeval innocence becomes translated into terms possible in the real world. For George and Lennie it becomes "a little house and a couple of acres." Out of this translation grows a second symbol, the rabbits, and this symbol serves several purposes. Through synecdoche it comes to stand for the "safe place" itself, making a much more easily manipulated symbol than the "house an' a couple of acres." Also, through Lennie's love for the rabbits Steinbeck is able not only to dramatize Lennie's desire for the "safe place," but to define the basis of that desire on a very low level of consciousness—the attraction to soft, warm fur, which is for Lennie the most important aspect of their plans.

This transference of symbolic value from the farm to the rabbits is important also because it makes possible the motif of action. This is introduced in the first scene by the dead mouse which Lennie is carrying in his pocket (much as Tom carries the turtle in *The Grapes of Wrath*). As George talks about Lennie's attraction to mice, it becomes evident that the symbolic rabbits will come to the same end—crushed by Lennie's simple, blundering strength. Thus Lennie's killing of mice and later his killing of the puppy set up a pattern which the reader expects to be carried out again. George's story about Lennie and the little girl with the red dress, which he tells twice, contributes to this expectancy of pattern, as do the shooting of Candy's dog, the crushing of Curley's hand, and the frequent appearances of Curley's wife. All these incidents are patterns of the action motif and predict the fate of the rabbits and thus the fate of the dream of a "safe place."

The third motif, that of language, is also present, in the opening scene. Lennie asks, George, "Tell me—like you done before," and George's words are obviously in the nature of a ritual. "George's voice became deeper. He repeated his words

rhythmically, as though he had said them many times before."
The element of ritual is stressed by the fact that even Lennie
has heard it often enough to remember its precise language:
"*An' live off the fatta the lan'* .... An' have *rabbits.* Go on George!
Tell about, what we're gonna have in the garden and about the
rabbits in the cages and about...." This ritual is performed often
in the story, whenever Lennie feels insecure. And of course it is
while Lennie is caught up in this dream vision that George
shoots him, so that on one level the vision is accomplished—
the dream never interrupted, the rabbits never crushed.

The highly patterned effect achieved by these incremental
motifs of symbol, action, and language is the knife-edge on
which criticism of *Of Mice and Men* divides. For although
Steinbeck's success in creating a pattern has been
acknowledged, criticism has been divided as to the effect of this
achievement. On one side, it is claimed that this strong
patterning creates a sense of contrivance and mechanical
action,[3] and on the other, that the patterning actually gives a
meaningful design to the story, a tone of classic fate.[4] What is
obviously needed here is some objective critical tool for
determining under what conditions a sense of inevitability (to
use a neutral word) should be experienced, as mechanical
contrivance, and when it should be experienced as catharsis
effected by a sense of fate. Such a tool cannot be forged within
the limits of this study; but it is possible to examine the
particular circumstances of *Of Mice and Men* more closely
before passing judgment.

Although the three motifs of symbol, action, and language
build up a strong pattern of inevitability, the movement is not
unbroken. About midway in the novel (chapters 3 and 4) there
is set up a countermovement which seems to threaten the
pattern. Up to this point the dream of "a house an' a couple of
acres" seemed impossible of realization. Now it develops that
George has an actual farm in mind (ten acres), knows the
owners and why they want to sell it: "The ol' people that owns
it is flat bust an' the ol' lady needs an operation." He even
knows the price—"six hundred dollars." Also, the old
workman, Candy, is willing to buy a share in the dream with

the three hundred dollars he has saved up. It appears that at the end of the month George and Lennie will have another hundred dollars and that quite possibly they "could swing her for that." In the following chapter this dream and its possibilities are further explored through Lennie's visit with Crooks, the power of the dream manifesting itself in Crooks's conversion from cynicism to optimism. But at the very height of his conversion the mice symbol reappears in the form of Curley's wife, who threatens the dream by bringing with her the harsh realities of the outside world and by arousing Lennie's interest.

The function of Candy's and Crooks's interest and the sudden bringing of the dream within reasonable possibility is to interrupt, momentarily, the pattern, of inevitability. But, and this is very important, Steinbeck handles this interruption so that it does not actually reverse the situation. Rather, it insinuates a possibility. Thus, though working against the pattern, this countermovement makes that pattern more credible by creating the necessary ingredient of free will. The story achieves power through a delicate balance of the protagonists' free will and the force of circumstance.

In addition to imposing a sense of inevitability, this strong patterning of events performs the important function of extending the story's range of meanings. This can best be understood by reference to Hemingway's "fourth dimension," which has been defined by Joseph Warren Beach as an "aesthetic factor" achieved by the protagonists' repeated participation in some traditional "ritual or strategy,"[5] and by Malcolm Cowley as "the almost continual performance of rites and ceremonies" suggesting recurrent patterns of human experience.[6] The incremental motifs of symbol, action, and language which inform *Of Mice and Men* have precisely these effects. The simple story of two migrant workers' dream of a safe retreat, a "clean well-lighted place," becomes itself a pattern of archetype which exists on three levels.

There is the obvious story level on a realistic plane, with its shocking climax. There is also the level of social protest,

Steinbeck the reformer crying out against the exploitation of migrant workers. The third level is an allegorical one, its interpretation limited only by the ingenuity of the audience. It could be, as Carlos Baker suggests, "an allegory of Mind and Body."[7] Using the same kind of dichotomy, the story could also be about the dumb, clumsy, but strong mass of humanity and its shrewd manipulators. This would make the book a more abstract treatment of the two forces of *In Dubious Battle*—the mob and its leaders. The dichotomy could also be that of the unconscious and the conscious, the id and the ego, or any other forces or qualities which have the same structural relationship to each other that do Lennie and George. It is interesting in this connection that the name Leonard means "strong or brave as a lion," and that the name George means "husbandman."

The title itself, however, relates the whole story to still another level which is implicit in the context of Burns's poem.

> *But, Mousie, thou art no thy lane,*
> *In proving foresight may be vain:*
> *The best laid schemes o' mice an' men*
> > *Gang aft a-gley*
> *An' lea'e us nought but grief an' pain*
> > *For promis'd joy.*

In the poem, Burns extends the mouse's experience to include that of mankind; in *Of Mice and Men*, Steinbeck extends the experience of two migrant workers to the human condition. "This is the way things are," both writers are saying. On this level, perhaps the most important, Steinbeck is dramatizing the non-teleological philosophy which had such a great part in shaping *In Dubious Battle* and which would be fully discussed in *Sea of Cortez*. This level of meaning is indicated by the title originally intended for the book—"Something That Happened."[8] In this light, the ending of the story is, like the ploughman's disrupting of the mouse's nest, neither tragic nor brutal, but simply a part of, the pattern of events. It is amusing in this regard that a Hollywood director suggested to Steinbeck that someone else kill the girl, so that sympathy could be kept with Lennie. (JS-MO, 3/?/38)

## Notes

3. Mark Van Doren, "Wrong Number," *The Nation*, 144 (March 6, 1937). p. 275; also, Joseph Wood Krutch, *American Drama Since 1918* (New York, 1939), p. 396.

4. Stark Young, "Drama Critics Circle Award," *The New Republic*, 94 (May 4, 1938), p. 396; also, Frank H. O'Hara, *Today in American Drama* (Chicago, 1939), p. 181.

5. "How Do You Like It Now, Gentlemen?" *Sewanee Review*, 59 (Spring, 1953.), pp. 311–328.

6. "Introduction," *The Portable Hemingway* (New York, 1944).

7. Carlos Baker, "Steinbeck of California," *Delphian Quarterly*, 23 (April, 1940), 42.

8. Toni Jackson Ricketts [Antonia Seixas], "John Steinbeck and the Non-Teleological Bus," *What's Doing on the Monterey Peninsula*, 3. (March, 1947). This article is now available in *Steinbeck and His Critics*, ed. by E. W. Tedlock, Jr., and C. V. Wicker (Albuquerque, 1957).

## WARREN FRENCH ON ARTHURIAN INFLUENCE AND ALLEGORY

Although other critics have not noted to what extent *Of Mice and Men* is an Arthurian story, the fundamental parallels—the knightly loyalty, the pursuit of the vision, the creation of a bond (shared briefly by Candy and Brooks), and its destruction by an at least potentially adulterous relationship—are there. They are, however, so concealed by the surface realism of the work that one unfamiliar with Steinbeck's previous Arthurian experiments would be hardly likely to notice them. The one obvious Arthurian hangover is George, who is not only remarkably loyal to his charge—the feeble-minded Lennie— but also remarkably pure.

George not only warns Lennie against the blandishments of Curley's wife, but is himself obviously impervious to her charms. While the other ranch hands are excited by her presence, George says only, "Jesus, what a tramp!" When invited to join the boys in a Saturday night trip to a neighboring town's "nicer" whorehouse, George says that he "might go in an' set and have a shot," but "ain't puttin' out no two and a half." He excuses himself on the ground that he is saving money to buy a farm, but not even Galahad might have found it politic to profess chastity in a bunkhouse. George seems to have stepped, in fact, not out of Malory's Arthurian stories but Tennyson's. When he is told that Curley boasts of having his glove full of Vaseline in order to keep his hand soft for his wife, George says, "That's a dirty thing to tell around."

George is noticeably more critical of Curley's wife than Steinbeck is. *Of Mice and Men* is not so completely objective as *In Dubious Battle*; Steinbeck editorializes occasionally, for example, after the girl has been killed:

> ... the meanness and the plannings and the discontent and the ache for attention were all gone from her face. She was very pretty and simple, and her face was sweet and young.

George shows no such sympathy, and it is important to notice that the author is more flexible than his character, because it is a sign that he is not being carried away by his vision as are the characters sometimes assumed to represent his viewpoint. The Arthurian flavor here is faint, but unmistakable. Like Jim Nolan, George is a last Galahad, dismounted, armed only with a fading dream, a long way from Camelot. Steinbeck is his historian, not his alter ego.

One does not need to justify a search for an allegory in *Of Mice and Men* since the author has spoken of the book as symbolic and microcosmic. Just what the universal drama enacted against a Salinas Valley backdrop may be is not, however, so obvious as first appears. Unquestionably it concerns a knight of low estate and a protégé who share a dream, a dream that cannot come true because the protégé lacks the mental capacity to be conscious enough to know his own strength or to protect himself from temptation.

At first glance, it appears that nature is the culprit and that this is an ironic, deterministic fable like Stephen Crane's "The Open Boat." It is an indifferent nature that makes men physically strong but mentally deficient; dreaming is man's only defense against a world he never made. "The best-laid schemes o' mice an' men gang aft agley," Burns said, providing Steinbeck with a title, because man is at the mercy of forces he cannot control which ruthlessly but indifferently destroy the illusions he has manufactured. The book may be read in this naturalistic manner, and those who speak of it as sentimental must think of it as an expression of Steinbeck's outraged compassion for the victims of chaotic forces.

Such a reading, however, does not do the story justice. If George stood helplessly by and saw Lennie destroyed, the novel might be called deterministic; but he doesn't. George has a will, and he exercises it to make two critical decisions at the end of the novel—to kill Lennie and to lie about it.

George could, of course, have killed Lennie simply to protect the giant brute from the mob; but, since Lennie doesn't know what is going on anyway, it is easy to oversentimentalize George's motives. Actually he has reasons of his own for pulling the trigger. Steinbeck makes it clear that George had tremendous difficulty bringing himself to destroy Lennie, although Lennie will not even know what has happened. What George is actually trying to kill is not Lennie, who is only a shell and a doomed one at that, but something in himself.

Peter Lisca points out that Lennie's need for George is obvious, but that George's need for Lennie, though less obvious, is as great. In his most candid appraisal of himself, George says, "I ain't so bright neither, or I wouldn't be buckin' barley for my fifty and found. If I was even a little bit smart, I'd have, my own little place..." He needs him, however, as more than just a rationalization for his own failure; for George not only protects but *directs* Lennie. Lennie doesn't speak unless George permits him to; and, in the fight in which Curley's hand is broken, Lennie refuses even to defend himself until George tells him to. George, of course, directs Lennie partly to protect him from committing acts he could not mentally be responsible for, but George is not a wholly altruistic shepherd.

Another aspect of the relationship becomes apparent when George tells Slim that Lennie, "Can't think of nothing to do himself, but he sure can take orders." Since George gives the orders, Lennie gives him a sense of power.

One aspect of the dream that George repeatedly describes to Lennie also needs scrutiny. The ritual ("George's voice became deeper. He repeated his words rhythmically.") begins "Guys like us, that work on ranches, are the loneliest guys in the world.... They ain't got nothing to look ahead to" and continues "with us it ain't like that ... because [here Lennie takes over from George] I got you to look after me, and you got me to look after you, and that's why." The dream not only gives a direction to their lives, but also makes them feel different from other people. Since this sense of difference can mean little to Lennie, it is part of the consolation George receives from the dream. George wants to be superior. With Lennie gone, his claim to distinction will be gone. Thus when George shoots Lennie, he is not destroying only the shared dream. He is also destroying the thing that makes him different and reducing himself to the status of an ordinary guy. He is obliged to acknowledge what Willy Loman in Arthur Miller's *Death of a Salesman*, for example, could never acknowledge but what Henry Morgan accepted when he turned respectable in *Cup of Gold*—his own mediocrity. George is much like Willy Loman; for he is forced to recognize the same self-deflating realization Biff Loman vainly tries to impress upon his father: he is a "dime a dozen." Because of their relationship, George has actually been able to remain as much a "kid" as Lennie; shooting him matures George in more than one way.

It is equally important that George lies to the posse after the shooting. If the experience had not matured him, he had here his opportunity for a grand gesture. He could either destroy himself along with Lennie and the dream or, by an impassioned confession, force his enemies to destroy him. George, who by Romantic standards has little left to live for, chooses to go on living and to say that he had to shoot Lennie in self-defense. Actually the maturing effect of the experience upon George has been apparent from the moment when, in reply to Candy's offer to help him carry out the dream, he says: "—I think I knowed from the very first. I think I know'd we'd never do her. He usta like to hear about it so much I got to thinking maybe we would." With Lennie gone, George will not try to keep the dream alive. When Slim leads George up toward the highway at the end of the novel, the wonder is not that George is badly shaken by his experience, but that he is alive at all.

Despite the grim events it chronicles *Of Mice and Men* is not a tragedy, but a comedy—which, if it were Shakespearean, we would call a "dark comedy"—about the triumph of the indomitable will to survive. This is a story not of man's defeat at the hands of an implacable nature, but of man's painful conquest of this nature and of his difficult, conscious rejection of his dreams of greatness and acceptance of his own mediocrity. Unfortunately, the allegory is less clear in the play version than in the novel, since Steinbeck, probably to provide a more effective curtain, eliminates George's last conversation with Slim and ends with the shooting of Lennie. The original ending would also probably have been too involved for playgoers to follow after experiencing the emotions engendered by the climactic episodes.

## WARREN FRENCH ON STEINBECK'S PHILOSOPHIES IN *OF MICE AND MEN*

Steinbeck's preoccupation with Ed Ricketts's non-teleological concepts that what things are matters less than the fact that they are led to the Naturalistic fable that precipitated the novelist into national celebrity, *Of Mice and Men*, which had once simply been titled "Something that Happened." This narrative differs from Steinbeck's earlier ones in that it was deliberately conceived as a novelette that might be turned without revision into a play. This unconventional idea was warmly greeted by a Broadway theater that was desperately searching for gimmicks that might help revive what was then known as "the fabulous invalid" laid low by the Depression and the competition from talking pictures. In fact, *Of Mice and Men* was staged the same season that Thornton Wilder's *Our Town* created a sensation by being played without scenery. When the short book became a Book-of-the-Month Club selection and a best seller, famed playwright and play-doctor George S. Kaufman helped Steinbeck prepare the acting version. Rights were sold to Hollywood; and, despite the censorship problems that the story posed in Hays Office days, it was finally—in the wake of the success of *The Grapes of Wrath*—turned into a powerful film.

Again, as in many of the short stories, a woman precipitates the tragic denouement; but this girl is herself—like Amy Hawkins in "Johnny Bear"—as much a victim as her victims. The real villain is her violent and insensitive husband; but he, too, cannot really be held responsible for the deaths at the end because he is scarcely more intelligent than the hulking innocent who becomes his prey. The whole affair is simply "something that happened"—all the characters find their world to be made of "oaths and walking-sticks," and their dreams are the only things that can keep them going. This view was likely to be particularly popular in the middle of the 1930s when many people regarded themselves as helpless victims of forces beyond their control. Many readers surely found easier identification with this story than with Steinbeck's earlier works since he wrote here not about an exotic ethnic group, as in *Tortilla Flat*, or about widely disliked "red" agitators, as in *In Dubious Battle*, but about rural American boys who, down on their luck, still dreamed the American dream of owning a little place of their own. "Nobody never gets to heaven; and nobody gets no land," Crooks, the Negro stable buck, observes cynically when he hears of George and Lennie's dream of owning a farm, and he summarizes the vision behind the work.

The action begins with George and Lennie, two itinerant ranch hands, who are preparing to start a new job. What differentiates this pair from the ordinary stumblebums then circulating the country in droves is the dream they share that George chants to Lennie's delight as they rest in a grove of willows: "Guys like us, that work on ranches, are the loneliest guys in the world. They got no family. They don't belong no place.... With us it ain't like that. We got a future...." At this point Lennie breaks in to help finish the familiar chant: "*because I got you to look after me, and you got me to look after you, and that's why.*" In the bunkhouse of their new employers, Slim, "a jerkline skinner, the prince of the ranch," observes that there "ain't many guys travel around together.... Maybe ever'body in the whole damn world is scared of each other."

George and Lennie have joined forces because, although George maintains that Lennie "ain't no cuckoo," he is undeniably overdeveloped physically and underdeveloped mentally—a powerful giant with an infant's brain. George has promised Lennie's aunt to look out for the giant; but, although George often complains of the demands that the commitment makes upon him, he derives from it the benefit of having someone to take care of and to share his dream of independence on a small ranch. This dream is sufficiently persuasive to win Candy, a handicapped bunkhouse swamper, whose old dog is killed by an unsentimental ranch hand who lives only by his sensations. The dream also tempts the cynical Negro Crooks out of the misanthropy resulting from his ostracism by the white hands.

The hopelessness of the dream is suggested, however, in the opening chapter when George and Lennie's conversation reveals that they have had to run away from their last job because of Lennie's supposedly molesting a girl. Lennie is also treasuring a dead mouse, for he loves to pet soft things. Because of his great strength and his lack of mental control, he unavoidably kills these things he loves; and, though George strives desperately to keep Lennie out of trouble, the dimwitted giant keeps finding mice, puppies, and girls to maul.

George senses trouble at the new location as soon as he meets Curley, the ranch-owner's son; a cocky lightweight fighter, he—as Candy explains—"hates big guys.... Kind of like he's mad at 'em because he ain't a big guy." Curley has recently married a girl whom Candy calls a "tart," and he is having trouble keeping track of her. Despite George's efforts, Curley picks a fight with Lennie and bloodies the giant's nose. Exasperated, George orders the reluctant Lennie to fight back, and Curley's hand is crushed. George and Lennie are afraid of losing their jobs, but Slim, the foreman, warns Curley that he will look ridiculous if his defeat is known.

Curley is silenced, but his wife is less easy to control. A restless, overpainted girl, her dreams of going to Hollywood have been encouraged by a casual date who took her to the cheap dancehall where she met Curley. Her intrusion into a Saturday night conversation between Lennie, Candy, and Crooks, after the hands have gone to town, is resented. Even though rejected by these "weak ones," she persists in forcing her attentions on Lennie on Sunday afternoon while the others are preoccupied by a horseshoe tournament. She gets Lennie to feel her soft hair; but, when he begins to muss it, she panics; and he breaks her neck.

We cannot sympathize with the girl. On Saturday night when Crooks tries to get her to leave the barn, she threatens him: "Well, you keep your place then, Nigger. I could get you strung up on a tree so easy it ain't even funny." Yet when she is dead, Steinbeck observes in one of the few departures from his dramatic objectivity in the narration: "Curley's wife lay with a half-covering of yellow hay. And the meanness and the plannings and the discontent and the ache for attention were all gone from her face. She was very pretty and simple, and her face was sweet and young. Now her rouged cheeks and her reddened lips made her seem alive and sleeping very lightly."

When George discovers what has happened, he realizes that his dream is ended. He pursues Lennie to a grove where they had agreed to meet should trouble develop. There, in a nightmarish sequence, George shoots Lennie before the other men, led by Curley—bent on lynching—can reach him. Although George's hand shakes violently, he sets his face and pulls the trigger; and, by doing so, he not only saves Lennie from the painful, but to him incomprehensible, vengeance of his pursuers, but also completely destroys the dream that has given George's own life a direction and meaning.

Slim, who comprehends the situation, consoles George by telling him that he had to do what he did; but the last word is assigned to the unfeeling dog-killer, who can only say with puzzlement, "Now what the hell ya suppose is eatin' them two guys." "The best laid schemes o' mice an' men / Gang aft a-gley" (in Robert Burns's familiar words) because even the man who has achieved a certain amount of control over his instincts and his fellowman—like George—is helpless in the hands of an indifferent, imperfect nature. Although the play follows the narrative of the novel, it misses this final point and stresses the sensational aspects of the plot by ending with the killing.

Slim's final attempt to console George ends the novel on the same compassionate note as that of *The Red Pony*, but Slim can only alleviate, not cure, the situation. A grown-up Jody Tiflin, he brings what comfort he can to one who has been obliged not just to witness the death of his dream but to strike the fatal blow himself. But *Of Mice and Men* is Steinbeck's last work for a long time to end on such a note of resignation. His next heroes—who truly merit that appellation—will make, even in going down to defeat, bold gestures that indicate that they intend to improve conditions or to die trying rather than "splitting up" before implacable forces or dying without recognizing the opponents they challenge.

## JOHN SEELYE ON CHARGES OF STEINBECK'S SENTIMENTALISM

Let us now turn to Steinbeck's other novels about dispossessed field workers, specifically to *Of Mice and Men*, which took its title from a beloved poem by Robert Burns, the Robert Frost of his own day and as often misconstrued. It is about a plowman who has turned up by accident a mouse's nest, and who, holding the quivering victim in his hand, philosophizes about the vicissitudes to which all living creatures are heir, and over which they have no control. Now there is a sadness that permeates much of Burns's poetry, he who wrote what might have served as the epithet for much sentimental literature, that "Man's inhumanity to man / Makes countless thousands mourn!" ("Man Was Made to Mourn" 56–57). And the image of the "wee, sleekit, cow'rin', tim'rous beastie" in "To a Mouse" with the "panic" in its "breastie" like Bambi is certainly susceptible to a sentimental reading (2). The plowman, holding the mouse, begs its pardon for having destroyed its home, for in asserting "Man's dominion," he has broken "Nature's social union" (7–8). But a companion poem is Burns's "To a Mountain Daisy," which contains the following stanza, starkly unsentimental and yet in keeping with the concluding line from "To a Mouse" that Steinbeck took as his title:

Ev'n thou who mourn'st the Daisy's fate,
That fate is thine—no distant date;
Stern Ruin's ploughshare drives elate
Full on thy bloom,
Till crush'd beneath the furrow's weight,
Shall be thy doom. (49–54)

*Of Mice and Men*, like the poem from which it takes its title, does seem susceptible to a sentimental reading. Fiedler's dismissive essay ignores Steinbeck's still highly popular novel, which enjoys sales of over 300,000 paperback copies a year, preferring for obvious reasons to attack *The Grapes of Wrath*, which sells only 150,000 copies a year. His preference gives heft to his notion that Steinbeck, like Dos Passos and James Farrell, is no longer read, as mythopoetic an idea as any conjured up by Edgar Rice Burroughs. But for our purposes, *Of Mice and Men* is particularly useful, not only because it is still widely read, but because, although it deals with the lives of migrant workers, it does not have a social agenda of any detectable kind. Indeed, from a modern, feminist perspective, it is probably Steinbeck's most politically incorrect work of fiction, errors of attitude that turn on the role played by the woman known only as Curley's wife, whose actions disrupt and finally destroy the vision of a male-centered paradise, the Edenic parable beneath the pastoral weave.

In Lennie and George we have a pair recalling the two men in Bret Harte's "Tennessee's Partner," in which male bonding is taken to a sentimental extreme. As in "The Luck of Roaring Camp," moreover, domesticity in this novel is identified with the male hegemony, for the Joad family's dream of owning a little farm is shared not only by Lennie and George but by the other migrant workers they are cast among, a green, pastoral hope we are called upon to share likewise, but which finally proves futile.

Likewise, Lennie's proclivity for taking up little furry creatures in his hand seems to be a sardonic reference to the sentimental plowman in Burns's poem, given what happens to them as a result. And when he holds and then crushes Curley's wife, we must I think regard him as a heedless and callous natural force, arbitrary and casual in its effects. Lennie's attraction to little furry things is sentimentality itself but what he does to them destroys the sentimental impulse along with the little furry thing. And when George administers an anaesthetic of sorts to Lennie, by pointing to the distant green prospect of their long deferred domestic paradise before shooting him, we have a perfect diagram of Steinbeck's use of the sentimental mode, which is to hold it out to us in a promising form and then, like Lennie with a wee mousie, crush it.

Steinbeck's is not, however, a cynical gesture. It is in keeping with his non-teleological view of the world, which is essentially unfriendly to linear and progressive literary forms, the kinds of discourse that sustain an argument or a thesis or a solution, whether it be Christian or Marxist doctrine. The sentimental mode, like the pastoral and epic with which it is often conjoined in protest novels, is one of the most linear of forms, pointing always to some happy and regenerative—even transfiguring—conclusion, and when used for the purpose of protest literature it holds out a socially determined solution to a social problem.

## LOUIS OWENS EXPLORES THE SIGNIFICANCE OF GEORGE AND LENNIE'S DREAM

The dream of George and Lennie represents a desire to defy the curse of Cain and fallen man—to break the pattern of

84

wandering and loneliness imposed on the outcasts and to return to the perfect garden. George and Lennie achieve all of this dream that is possible in the real world: they are their brother's keeper. Unlike the solitary Cain and the solitary men who inhabit the novel, they have someone who cares. The dream of the farm merely symbolizes their deep mutual commitment, a commitment that is immediately sensed by the other characters in the novel. The ranch owner is suspicious of the relationship, protesting, "I never seen one guy take so much trouble for another guy" (p. 25). Slim, the godlike jerkline skinner, admires the relationship and says, "Ain't many guys travel around together.... I don't know why. Maybe everybody in the whole damn world is scared of each other" (p. 43). Candy, the one-handed swamper, and Crooks, the deformed black stablehand, also sense the unique commitment between the two laborers, and in their moment of unity Candy and Crooks turn as one to defend Lennie from the threat posed by Curley's wife. The influence of George and Lennie's mutual commitment, and of their dream, has for an instant made these crippled sons of Cain their brother's keepers and broken the grip of loneliness and solitude in which they exist. Lennie's yearning for the rabbits and for all soft, living things symbolizes the yearning all men have for warm, living contact. It is this yearning, described by Steinbeck as "the inarticulate and powerful yearning of all men,"[31] which makes George need Lennie just as much as Lennie needs George and which sends Curley's wife wandering despairingly about the ranch in search of companionship. Whereas Fontenrose has suggested that "the individualistic desire for carefree enjoyment of pleasures is the serpent in the garden" in this book,[32] the real serpent is loneliness and the barriers between men and between men and women that create and reinforce this loneliness.

Lennie has been seen as representing "the frail nature of primeval innocence"[33] and as the id to George's ego or the body to George's brain.[34] In the novel, Lennie is repeatedly associated with animals or described as childlike. He appears in the opening scene dragging his feet "the way a bear drags his paws" (p. 2), and in the final scene he enters the clearing in the brush "as silently as a creeping bear" (p. 110). Slim says of Lennie, "He's jes' like a kid, ain't he," and George repeats, "Sure, he's jes' like a kid" (p. 48). The unavoidable truth is, however, that Lennie, be he innocent "natural," uncontrollable id, or simply a huge child, is above all dangerous. Unlike Benjy in *The Sound and the Fury* (whom Steinbeck may have had in mind when describing the incident in Weed in which Lennie clings bewildered to the girl's dress), Lennie is monstrously powerful and has a propensity for killing things. Even if Lennie had not killed Curley's wife, he would sooner or later have done something fatal to bring violence upon himself, as the lynch mob that hunted him in Weed suggests.

Steinbeck's original title for *Of Mice and Men* was "Something That Happened," a title suggesting that Steinbeck was taking a purely non-teleological or non-blaming point of view in this novel. If we look at the novel in this way, it becomes clear that Lennie dies because he has been created incapable of dealing with society and is, in fact, a menace to society. Like Pepé in "Flight," Tularecito in *The Pastures of Heaven*, and Frankie in *Cannery Row*, Lennie is a "natural" who loses when he is forced to confront society. This is simply the way it is—something that happened—and when George kills Lennie he is not only saving him from the savagery of the pursuers, he is, as John Ditsky says, acknowledging that "Lennie's situation is quite hopeless." Ditsky further suggests that Lennie's death represents "a matter of cold hard necessity imposing itself upon the frail hopes of man." Along these same lines, Joan Steele declares that "Lennie has to be destroyed because he is a "loner" whose weakness precludes his cooperating with George and hence working constructively toward their mutual goal."[35] Lennie, however, is not a "loner"; it is, in fact, the opposite, overwhelming and uncontrollable urge for contact that brings about Lennie's destruction and the destruction of living creatures he comes into contact with. Nonetheless, Steele makes an important point when she suggests that because of Lennie the dream of the Edenic farm was never a possibility. Lennie's flaw represents the inherent imperfection in humanity that renders Eden forever an impossibility. Lennie would have brought his imperfection with him to the little farm, and he would have killed the rabbits.

When Lennie dies, the teleological dream of the Edenic farm dies with him, for while Lennie's weakness doomed the dream it was only his innocence that kept it alive. The death of the dream, however, does not force *Of Mice and Men* to end on the strong note of pessimism critics have consistently claimed. For while the dream of the farm perishes, the theme of commitment achieves its strongest statement in the book's conclusion. Unlike Candy, who abandons responsibility for his old dog and allows Carlson to shoot him, George remains his brother's keeper without faltering even to the point of killing Lennie while Lennie sees visions of Eden. In accepting complete responsibility for Lennie, George demonstrates the degree of commitment necessary to the Steinbeck hero, and in fact enters the ranks of those heroes. It is ironic that, in this fallen world, George must reenact the crime of Cain to demonstrate the depth of his commitment. It is a frank acceptance of the way things are.

Slim recognizes the meaning of George's act. When the pursuers discover George just after he has shot Lennie, Steinbeck writes: "Slim came directly to George and sat down beside him, sat very close to him" (pp. 118–19). Steinbeck's forceful prose here, with the key word "directly," and the emphatic repetition in the last phrase place heavy emphasis on Slim's gesture. Steinbeck is stressing the significance of the new relationship between George and Slim. As the novel ends, George is going off with Slim to have a drink, an action Fontenrose mistakenly interprets as evidence "that George had turned to his counter-dream of independence: freedom from Lennie." French suggests that "Slim's final attempt to console George ends the novel on the same compassionate note as that of *The Red Pony*, but Slim can only alleviate, not cure, the situation."[36] Steinbeck, however, seems to be deliberately placing much greater emphasis on the developing friendship between the two men than such interpretations would allow for. Lisca has pointed out the circular structure of the novel—the neat balancing of the opening and closing scenes. Bearing this circularity in mind, it should be noted that this novel about man's loneliness and "apartness" began with two men—George and Lennie—climbing down to the pool from the highway and that the novel ends with two men—George and Slim—climbing back up from the pool to the highway. Had George been left alone and apart from the rest of humanity at the end of the novel, had he suffered the fate of Cain, this would indeed have been the most pessimistic of Steinbeck's works. That George is not alone has tremendous significance. In the fallen world of the valley, where human commitment is the only realizable dream, the fact that in the end as in the beginning two men walk together causes *Of Mice and Men* to end on a strong note of hope—the crucial dream, the dream of man's commitment to man, has not perished with Lennie. The dream will appear again, in fact, in much greater dimension in Steinbeck's next novel, *The Grapes of Wrath*.

## Notes

31. Steinbeck is quoted in Fontenrose, *John Steinbeck: An Introduction and Interpretation*, p. 57.

32. Ibid., p. 59.

33. Astro, *Steinbeck and Ricketts*, p. 104.

34. Lisca, *John Steinbeck: Nature and Myth*, pp. 78–79.

35. John Ditsky, "Ritual Murder in Steinbeck's Dramas," *Steinbeck Quarterly* 11 (Summer–Fall 1978): 73; Joan Steele, "A Century of Idiots: *Barnaby Rudge* and *Of Mice and Men*," *Steinbeck Quarterly* 5 (Winter 1972): 16.

36. Fontenrose, *John Steinbeck: An Introduction and Interpretation*, p. 57; French, *John Steinbeck*, 2d ed., p. 91.

## HOWARD LEVANT EXPLAINS HOW THE NOVEL'S FORM SHOWS STEINBECK'S SKILL

Despite Steinbeck's disclaimer in *Stage*, *Of Mice and Men*[7] is certainly a play-novelette according to Steinbeck's own theory. Biographical information supports this view. Steinbeck reported to his agents, at the beginning of his work in February

1935, "I'm doing a play now," and Harry Thornton Moore records several illuminating contemporary facts:

> After *Of Mice and Men* was published and the suggestion was made that it be prepared for the stage, Steinbeck said it could be produced directly from the book, as the earliest moving pictures had been produced. It was staged in almost exactly this way in the spring of 1937 by a labor-theater group in San Francisco, and although the venture was not a failure it plainly demonstrated to Steinbeck that the story needed to be adapted to dramatic form.... But when Steinbeck transferred the story into final dramatic form for the New York stage he took 85% of his lines bodily from the novel. A few incidents needed juggling, one or two minor new ones were introduced, and some (such as Lennie's imaginary speech with his Aunt Clara at the end of the novel) were omitted.[8]

It would seem that the novel was intended to function as a play, and Steinbeck did not alter the novel in any essential during the tinkering in preparation for the New York stage production. Aesthetic considerations support the biographical information, as in Moore's observation:

> Structurally, the novel was from the first a play: it is divided into six parts, each part a scene—the reader may observe that the action never moves away from a central point in each of these units.[9]

And clearly the novel does "play": Characters make entrances and exits; plainly indicated parallels and oppositions that are characteristic of the drama exist in quantity and function as they should; suspense is maintained; characters are kept uncomplicated and "active" in the manner of stage characterization; since there is little internal or implicit development, events depend on what is said or done in full view; the locale is restricted mainly to one place; the span of time is brief; the central theme is stated and restated—the good life is impossible because humanity is flawed—and in itself is deeply poignant, as Steinbeck had defined a play-novelette theme. In short, I do not see how *Of Mice and Men* could meet more completely the specifications of a play-novelette as Steinbeck listed them. If critics have been displeased with *Of Mice and Men*, as Steinbeck was, the trouble cannot lie in the application of the theory but in the assumption that inspired the theory. I shall explore this point in detail.

As a dramatic structure, *Of Mice and Men* is focused on Lennie and occurs within the context of the bunkhouse and the ranch. Within these confines, Steinbeck develops theme and countertheme by exploring the chances for the good life against the flawed human material that Lennie symbolizes most completely and the code of rough justice that most people accept. Even this initial, limited statement points to the central difficulty in the novel. The "well-made" dramatic form that Steinbeck defined in *Stage* and did construct in *Of Mice and Men* is conducive to abstraction because it is limited to visible action. Lennie is limited in much the same way. As a huge, powerful, semi-idiot who kills when he is frightened or simply when he is thoughtless, Lennie is a reduction of humanity to the lowest common denominator. It may be possible to construct a parable out of so limited a structure and materials, but it is impossible to handle complex human motives and relationships within those limits. *Of Mice and Men* is successful to the extent that it remains a parable, but the enveloping action is more complex than the parable form can encompass.

Lennie is the most fully realized character, yet he is presented necessarily as a personification, an exaggerated, allegorized instance of the division between mind and body; the sketch that is Lennie is incapable of conveying personality. The other characters are personified types rather than realized persons. Though less pathetic than Lennie, they do not have his moral impact. In short, every structural device except personification is sacrificed to highlight Lennie's moral helplessness. The sacrifice is much too great. It thins out the parable. The stripped language furthers this effect of extreme thinness. For example, Lennie's one friend, George, is not a realized man but a quality that complements Lennie's childlike innocence. George fills out Lennie's pattern to complete a whole man. He is a good man, motivated to protect Lennie because he realizes that Lennie is the reverse image of his own human nature. George is a representation of humanity that (unlike Lennie) is aware of evil. An extended abstract passage (pages 70–76), makes this clear.

Everything in the development of the novel is designed to contribute to a simplification of character and event.

The opening scene of the green pool in the Salinas River promises serenity, but in the final scene the pool is the background for Lennie's violent death. George's initial hope that Lennie can hide his flawed humanity by seeming to be conventional is shattered in the end. Lennie's flaw grows into a potential for evil, and every evil is ascribed to him after his unwitting murder of Curley's wife. The objective image of the good life in the future, "a little house and a couple of acres an' a cow and some pigs," is opposed sharply to the present sordid reality of the bunkhouse and the ranch.[10] Minor characters remain little more than opposed types, identifiable by allegorical tags. Curley is the unsure husband, opposed to and fearful of his sluttish, unnamed wife. Slim is a minor god in his perfect mastery of his work. His serenity is contrasted sharply with Curley's hysterical inability to please or to control his wife, and it contrasts as easily with the wife's constant, obvious discontent. Candy and Crooks are similar types, men without love. Both are abused by Curley, his wife, and the working crew. (Lennie might fall into this category of defenselessness, if he were aware enough to realize the situation; but he is not.) These sharp oppositions and typed personae restrict the development of the novel. The merely subordinate characters, such as Carlson and Whit, who only begin or fill out a few scenes, are strictly nonhuman, since they remain abstract instruments within a design.

The climax of that design is simplified in its turn, since it serves only to manipulate Lennie into a moral situation beyond his understanding. The climax is doubled, a pairing of opposites. In its first half, when Curley's wife attempts to seduce Lennie as a way to demonstrate her hatred of Curley, Lennie is content (in his nice innocence) to stroke her soft hair; but he is too violent, and he snaps her neck in a panic miscalculation as he tries to force her to be quiet. In the second half, George shoots Lennie to prevent a worse death at the hands of others. The melodramatic quality of these events will be considered at a later point. Here, it is more important to observe, in the design, that the climax pairs an exploration of the ambiguity of love in the rigid contrast between the different motives that activate Curley's wife and George. Curley's wife wants to use Lennie to show her hatred for Curley; George shoots Lennie out of a real affection for him. The attempted seduction balances the knowing murder; both are disastrous expressions of love. Lennie is the unknowing center of the design in both halves of this climax. Steinbeck's control is all too evident. There is not much sense of dramatic illumination because the quality of the paired climax is that of a mechanical problem of joining two parallels. Lennie's necessary passivity enforces the quality of a mechanical design. He is only the man to whom things happen. Being so limited, he is incapable of providing that sudden widening insight which alone justifies an artist's extreme dependence on a rigid design. Therefore, in general, *Of Mice and Men* remains a simple anecdote.

It would be a mistake to conclude that the limited scope of the materials is the only or the effective cause of the simplification. Writers frequently begin their work with anecdotal materials. Most often, however, they expand the reference of such materials through a knowing exercise of their medium.[11] It is Steinbeck's inability to exercise his medium or, perhaps more fundamentally, to select a proper medium, which ensures the limited reference, the lack of a widening insight.

In his discussion of the play-novelette form in *Stage*, Steinbeck dismisses the objection that allegory is an overly limited form,[12] but the objection is serious. *Of Mice and Men* is not merely a brief novel. It is limited in what its structure can make of its materials. Moreover, Steinbeck hoped to achieve precisely that limitation—the *Stage* essay leaves no doubt of this—although, it is true, he felt the form would ensure a concentration, a focus, of the materials. Instead, there is a deliberate thinning of materials that are thin (or theatrical) to begin with.

In fact, Steinbeck uses every possible device to thin out the effect of the materials. Foreshadowing is overworked. Lennie's murder of Curley's wife is the catastrophe that George has been dreading from the start. It is precisely the fate that a fluffy animal like Curley's wife should meet at the hands of Lennie, who has already killed mice and a puppy with his overpowering tenderness.[13] When Curley's wife makes clear her intention to seduce the first available man and the course of events abandons Lennie to her, the result is inevitable. But that inevitability does not have tragic qualities. The result is merely arranged, the characters merely inarticulate, and the action develops without illumination. Lennie can hardly distinguish between a dead pup and the dead woman:

> Lennie went back and looked at the dead girl. The puppy lay close to her. Lennie picked it up. "I'll throw him away," he said. "It's bad enough like it is."[14]

The relative meaninglessness of his victims substitutes pathos for tragedy. Curley's rather shadowy wife underlines the substitution: She is characterless, nameless, and constantly discontent, so her death inspires none of the sympathy one might feel for a kind or a serene woman. Others respond to her death wholly in light of Lennie's predicament—from George's loving concern to Curley's blustering need for revenge—not his character. Everything that is excellent in the novel tends to relate, intensely if narrowly, to that emphasis. Within these limits, much that Steinbeck does is done excellently. The essential question is whether the treatment of the materials is intense enough to justify their evident manipulation, their narrowed pathos.

The novel communicates most intensely a theme of unconventional morality. Lennie does commit murder, but he remains guiltless because he is not responsible for what he does.[15] Yet the morality is only a statement of the pathos of Lennie's situation, not an exploration of guilt and innocence. A development through parallels and juxtapositions does little to expand the stated theme. Carlson parallels Lennie's violence on a conventional level when he insists on killing Candy's ancient, smelly dog. Carlson's reasoning is that the group has a right to wrong the individual. Lennie is incapable of any logic, even of this twisted sort, and he is never cruel by choice; that potential moral complexity is neglected in the design to permit the brutal simplicity of the group's response to Carlson's argument and to Lennie's crime. Carlson's crime is approved by the group: He abuses power to invade another man's desire for affection, reduced to a worthless dog. Lennie's crime is an accident in an attempt to express affection; murder is too serious for the group to ignore, so Lennie is hunted down. We are intended to notice the irony that Carlson's crime inverts Lennie's. That simple, paralleled irony substitutes for a possible, intense, necessarily complex, and ambiguous development of the materials. The rendered development, not the materials themselves, produces this simply mechanical irony.

Certainly the theme of unconventional morality offers tragic possibilities in a dimension beyond the anecdotal or the sketch of a character or event. From that viewpoint, the oppositions can expand into tragic awareness, at least potentially. They can even be listed, as follows. Lennie is good in his intentions, but evil in fact. The group is good in wanting to punish a murderer, but evil in misunderstanding that Lennie is guiltless. Counterwise, George, Candy, and Slim are endowed with understanding by their roles as the friend, the man without hope, and the god, but they are powerless against the group. Curley's wife is knowingly evil in exploiting Lennie's powerful body and weak mind. Curley is evil in exploiting all opportunities to prove his manhood. These two are pathetic in their human limitations, not tragic. George enacts an unconventional morality less by accident than any of the others. He feels strongly that, in being compelled to look after Lennie, he has given up the good times he might have had, but he knows the sacrifice is better, that he and Lennie represent an idealized variety of group-man. Slim's early, sympathetic insight makes this explicit:

> "You guys travel around together?" [Slim's] tone was friendly. It invited confidence without demanding it. "Sure," said George. "We kinda look after each other." He indicated Lennie with his thumb. "He ain't bright. Hell of a good worker, though. Hell of a nice fella, but he ain't bright. I've knew him for a long time." Slim looked through George and beyond him. "Ain't many guys travel around together," he mused. "I don't know why. Maybe ever'body in the whole damn world is scared of each other." "It's a lot nicer to go around with a guy you know," said George.[16]

This important passage centers the theme of unconventional morality. It celebrates a relationship "the whole damn world" is incapable of imagining, given the ugly context of ranch life and sordid good times, and it locates the good life in friendship, not in the material image of the little farm. This passage is the heart of the novel.

But a novel cannot be structured solely on the basis of a theme, even a fundamental theme. Too much else must be simplified. Worse, the unconventional morality located in friendship produces Lennie's death, not only because Steinbeck can see no other way to conclude. Lennie dies necessarily because friendship can go no further than it does go, and nothing can be made of the dreamlike ideal of the little farm. The extreme simplification is that Steinbeck can do nothing with Lennie after he has been exhibited. These limitations derive from the simplification required by the play-novelette form. Steinbeck appears to be aware that formal limitations need some widening, since he imbeds Lennie's happiest and most intense consciousness of the good life of friends in an ironic context:

> George said, "Guys like us got no fambly. They make a little stake an then they blow it in. They ain't got nobody

in the worl' that gives a hoot in hell about 'em—" "*But not us*," Lennie cried happily. "Tell about us now." George was quiet for a moment. "But not us," he said. "Because—" "Because I got you an'—" "An' I got you. We got each other, that's what, that gives a hoot in hell about us," Lennie cried in triumph.[17]

The passage extends friendship beyond its boundary; it celebrates a species of marriage, minus the sexual element, between Lennie and George. But the content of the passage is qualified heavily by its position; George shoots Lennie after retelling the story about the little farm that always quiets Lennie. As further irony, precisely the responsibilities of a perfect friendship require George to shoot Lennie. The mob that would hang Lennie for murder is in the background throughout the scene. The situation is moving, but the effect is local. The ironies relate only to Lennie's pathetic situation; they do not aid an understanding of Lennie or account (beyond plot) for his death. Too, the scene is melodramatic; it puts aside the large problems of justifying the event in order to jerk our tears over the event itself.

To say that Steinbeck avoids the problems of structure by milking individual scenes is not to say that *Of Mice and Men* is a total failure. As mature work, it is not a depot for the basic flaws in Steinbeck's earliest work. Many of the scenes are excellently constructed and convincing in themselves. Considerable attention is given to establishing minor details. For example, George shoots Lennie with the Luger that Carlson used to kill Candy's old dog. The defenseless man is linked by the weapon with the defenseless dog in the group's web of created power. George does his killing as a kind of ritual. If the police or the mob had taken Lennie, the death would have been a meaningless expression of group force, the exaction of an eye for an eye rather than an expression of love. The background of language is the workingman dialect that Steinbeck perfected in *In Dubious Battle*, realized here to express a brutally realistic world that negates idealism and exaggerates the sadistic and the ugly. Its perfection is enhanced by a factual context—the dependence of the men on their shifting jobs, the explicit misery of their homelessness, and the exposure of their social and economic weaknesses. The more sensitive men dream of escape into some kind of gentleness. The thread of possible realization of that dream tends to hold the novel in a focus. The opposite pole of man's imperfect moral nature motivates Curley's wife and Carlson. Steinbeck's fine web of circumstance reaches from the ideal possibility to the brutal fact.

*Of Mice and Men* is strongest in precisely this plot sense, in a sequence and linkage of events controlled by ironic contrast and juxtaposition. The result is limited to the rendering of a surface, yet the necessarily external devices of plot are used with artistic care and skillful tact.

Just after George, Lennie, and Candy agree to realize the dream of the little farm by pooling their savings and earnings, Curley appears, searching for his wife. Frustrated, Curley punches Lennie without mercy until (on George's order) Lennie grabs and crushes Curley's hand. This violent event suggests that Curley's sadistic vision of the world will not be shut out by the idealized vision of cooperative friends. More closely, the ugly inversion of "the good, clean fight" serves to contrast Lennie's innocence with his surprise and helplessness before evil. The other men in the bunkhouse are unconcerned; violence is an ordinary element in their lives. The incident enacts and announces the implicitly universal moral imperfection of humanity—an insight that broadens and becomes more overt in the following scenes. When Curley has to go to town to have a doctor care for his crushed hand, the men take the chance to go into town for a spree. Crooks, Candy, and Lennie—the Negro, the old man, and the idiot— are left on the ranch with Curley's wife. The circumstances provide her with an opportunity to seduce Lennie; she hates Curley, and the Hollywood ideal of the seductive movie queen is her only standard of love. Crooks cannot protect Lennie because his black skin leaves him open to sexual blackmail; Candy's feeble efforts are useless; and Lennie does not understand what is happening. The ultimate irony in this tangle of violence is that none of the characters is evil or intends to do evil. The irony is more explicit and more powerful than the crux of the Munroe family in *The Pastures of Heaven*, in that all of them are trying to express some need of love. In her need as in her amoral unawareness of good and evil, Curley's wife is not unlike Lennie, just as the various moral defects of other people conspire by chance to leave Lennie alone and defenseless with Curley's wife. Yet "love" has different meanings for Lennie and for Curley's wife; the clash of meanings ensures their deaths.

The death of Curley's wife switches the narrative focus to George and to the device of the split hero. Steinbeck is fond of this device of a divided (not a duplicated) hero, usually two men of opposite nature, one distinctly secondary to the other, but both sharing the center of the novel. For a few suggestive, not inclusive, examples: Henry Morgan, Jim Nolan, and Aaron Trask are coldly thoughtful, knowing men, either selfish or idealistic in what they do; Coeur de Gris, Mac, and Caleb Trask are relatively warmer men, possibly as knowing as their opposites, but usually more subject to their emotions. Jim Casy and Tom Joad extend and complicate the pattern as they become suggestive types of Christ and Saint Paul, the human god and the coldly realistic organizer, but they do not break the pattern. There are obvious narrative virtues of clarity in a device that is recognizable as well as flexible. The secondary hero is subordinate in Steinbeck's fiction—except in *Of Mice and Men*. There, Lennie's murder propels George into a sudden prominence that has no structural basis. Is the novel concerned with Lennie's innocence or George's guilt? The formal requirements of a play-novelette mandate a structural refocus. Steinbeck needs a high point to ring down the curtain. With Lennie dead, Steinbeck must use and emphasize George's guilt. The close is formulated—the result of a hasty switch—not structured from preceding events, so it produces an inconclusive ending in view of what has happened previously. And the ideal of the farm vanishes with Lennie's death, when George tells Candy the plan is off.

Here the difficulty is with a structure that requires a climax which cannot be achieved once Lennie, the center of the novel, is removed; but Lennie must be killed off when his existence raises problems of characterization more complex than the play-novelette form can express. Materials and structure pull against each other and finally collapse into an oversimplified conclusion that removes rather than faces the central theme.

The abrupt "solution" rests on melodrama, on sudden, purely plot devices of focus and refocus. Such overt manipulation indicates that in its practice the play-novelette is not a new form. Steinbeck's experience, his mature technical skill do not finally disguise his wish to return to his earliest fictional efforts to realize complex human behavior by way of an extreme simplification of structure and materials. His deliberate avoidance of an organic structure and his consequent dependence on a formula, on the exercise of technique within an artistic vacuum, exhausts the significance of the play-novelette theory. His practice, as in *Of Mice and Men*, does not lead to serious efforts and to a real achievement in the art of the novel. Rather, it leads to manipulations designed to effect a simplification of structure and materials. So much skill, directed toward so little, is disturbing. But the skill is absolutely there.

## Notes

7. John Steinbeck, *Of Mice and Men* (New York: Covici, Friede, Inc., 2937). Hereafter cited as *OMM*.

8. Moore, p. 49; Lisca, p. 230.

9. Moore, p. 48.

10. *OMM*, pp. 28–30, 60.

11. Mark Schorer, "Technique as Discovery," *Hudson Review*, 1 (Spring 1948), 67–87. I am much indebted to Schorer's argument.

12. *Stage*, p. 51.

13. *OMM*, pp. 15, 151.

14. *OMM*, p. 159.

15. This paradox is the "moral" of the poem by Robert Burns which supplies the title of the novel; the title indicates Steinbeck's own concentration on a thematic development, not on characters or events as important in themselves. Further: A "moral" does tend to be simple.

16. *OMM*, pp. 63–64. After Lennie's death, Slim invites George to go into town, to enjoy the good times now in reach (drinking, gambling, whoring). From the weary tone of aftermath, these good times are clearly an entirely inadequate substitute for friendship. Yet the special world of Mack and the boys (in *Cannery Row*) has its creative basis in this passage. Steinbeck protects and ensures the survival of that later world precisely by making it special—and somewhat incredible, or overly simple, even on its own terms. Steinbeck can destroy or sentimentalize; his treatment of such materials occurs within those limits.

17. *OMM*, pp. 180–81. This is a repetition of an earlier passage in a less sinister context (pp. 28–29). Compare the close of *In Dubious Battle*.

# WARREN FRENCH DISCUSSES PESSIMISM AND CROOKS

The pessimistic vision behind the tale is articulated by a crippled stablebuck, Crooks—one of the few important black characters in Steinbeck's fiction—who lives in lonely isolation, ostracized from the communal bunkhouse. In an attack on the proletarian novelists' vision of a worker's paradise, Crooks explains, "I seen hunderds of men come by on the road an' on the ranches, with their bindles on their back an' that same damn thing in their heads.... [E]very damn one of 'ems got a little piece of land in his head. An' never a God damn one of 'em ever gets it. Just like heaven.... Nobody ever gets to heaven, and nobody gets no land."[3]

Critics have made efforts to argue that the ending of the novel, when Slim, the wise foreman at the ranch, takes George up the trail for a drink, offers a ray of hope that makes this story less defeatist than *Tortilla Flat* and *In Dubious Battle*. Steinbeck gives the last word not to Slim, however, but to the insensitive owner of the Luger—with all its fascist symbolism—who says to the sadistic Curley, "Now what the hell ya suppose is eatin' them two guys?" Steinbeck is still presenting an unfeeling world where any sign of human caring is exploited as a weakness. Slim can understand situations and momentarily ameliorate them, but he cannot cure them. George has been forced to destroy by his own hand a dream that cannot be revived.

Few comments by Steinbeck while writing this work have been published, but a remarkable letter that he wrote to actress Claire Luce while she was playing Curley's wife on Broadway shows much about his detailed conception of characters that can only be hinted at in published texts, as well as about the misanthropic mood he was in while composing this work. A member of his agents' staff had written him that the actress was beginning to have misgivings about her interpretation of the part. Steinbeck pointed out that "she was trained by threat not only at home but by other kids.... She learned she had to be hard to cover her fright.... She is a nice, kind girl and not a floozy. No man has ever considered her as anything except a girl to make.... She is afraid of everyone in the world.... [Girls like that] pretend to be wise and hard and voluptuous" (*Life*, 155).

While he was writing this novel, Steinbeck had just been through problems over the acceptance of *In Dubious Battle*, he was uncomfortable and frightened himself by celebrity, a puppy had destroyed about two months' work on the book, he was depressed as his success made old friends envious, and he had to project a tough image to protect himself from importunings. His letter to Claire Luce suggests that he was again projecting many of his own problems through his characters'. The world as he saw it at this point was dominated by the unfeeling Curleys and Carlsons, and there was no resting place before the grave for innocents like Curley's wife or George and Lennie.

Perhaps this is a young person's book after all—not for small children but for teenagers (and it has become one of the most widely used modern novels in high schools)—precisely because of its disillusioning message that dreams can be dangerous and destructive. Steinbeck's own next effort was to try to write a book in which from his own report he tried to be wise and hard, but he could not go through with its publication. Instead he wrote *The Grapes of Wrath*.

**Note**

3. *Of Mice and Men* (New York: Covici, Friede, 1937), 129–30.

## JOHN TIMMERMAN ON LOCATIONS AND FRAMES IN THE NOVEL

The novel opens with the objective specificity of locale that would mark stage directions, or perhaps cinema. Like a long pan of the camera, the opening scene traces the Salinas River where it "drops in close to the hillside bank and runs deep and green" near Soledad. Following the flow of the river, the scene narrows and becomes more specific in detail, moving from the broad expanse of the "golden foothill slopes" of the Gabilan Mountains to the very small setting of "the sandy bank under the trees," where we find details as minute as "a lizard makes a great skittering" and "the split-wedge tracks of deer." The narrowing vision provides a smooth and gentle transition to the two bindlestiffs hunkered by a fire in the evening of the day. The light, too, narrows and focuses, from the broad, golden flanks of the Gabilans to the evening duskiness and the shade "that climbed up the hills toward the top."

The expertly framed opening is precisely echoed and inverted at the close of the novel, where the same two bindlestiffs stand by "the deep green pool of the Salinas River" in the evening of the day. Once again shade pushes the sunlight "up the slopes of the Gabilan Mountains, and the hilltops were rosy in the sun." We find the same, familiarly routine skitterings of birds and animals by the sandy bank, only now a small something has happened. The original title of the novel, "Something That Happened," is precisely the point here; a small thing occurs, however momentous and tragic in the lives of Lennie and George, that goes virtually unnoticed in the ways of the world. Antonia Seixas comments in her article "John Steinbeck and the Non-Teleological Bus" that "the hardest task a writer can set himself is to tell the story of 'something that happened' without explaining 'why'—and make it convincing and moving."[30] Again, as if viewing the scene through a movie camera, we observe the "what" without the explanatory "why." While Lennie stares into the sun-washed mountains, George recreates the dream as he levels the Luger at the base of Lennie's skull.

The mountains that frame the story, as they frame the little thing that happened in the lives of George and Lennie, always carry large significance for Steinbeck. In *The Grapes of Wrath* crossing the mountains represents the entrance into the promised land for the Okies. In *East of Eden*, Steinbeck provides two mountain ranges, one dark and one light, which symbolically frame the struggle between good and evil in the valley between those ranges. In *The Red Pony*, as in *To a God Unknown*, the mountains represent mystery; in the former work old Gitano goes to the mountains on Easter to die; in the latter Joseph Wayne witnesses strange, ancient rituals. In *Of Mice and Men* also, the darkening mountains represent the mystery of death, carefully sustained in the minor imagery of the heron seizing and eating the little water snakes.

In between the two scenes of the mountains on those two evenings, and in the serene willow grove that, as Peter Lisca points out, symbolizes "a retreat from the world to a primeval innocence,"[31] we have the quiet drama of George and Lennie's dream unfolding and unraveling. But this dream is doomed, and Steinbeck provides ample foreshadowing in the novel, most notably in Candy's dog. According to Carlson, Candy's dog has to die because he is a cripple, out of sorts with the normal routine of society, something in the way. With careful detail Carlson describes how he would shoot the dog so that it would not feel any pain: "'The way I'd shoot him, he wouldn't feel nothing. I'd put the gun right there.' He pointed with his toe. 'Right back of the head. He wouldn't even quiver'" (p. 82). Candy's huge regret is that he didn't do so himself. It would have been kinder to have the dog die by a familiar and loved hand than to have a stranger drag him to his death. The same feeling motivates George as he leads the social cripple Lennie to his dream world. For Steinbeck this act constitutes a rare heroism. Years later he wrote in a letter to Annie Laurie Williams:

M & M may seem to be unrelieved tragedy, but it is not. A careful reading will show that while the audience knows, against its hopes, that the dream will not come true, the protagonists must, during the play, become convinced that it will come true. Everyone in the world has a dream he knows can't come off but he spends his life hoping it may. This is at once the sadness, the greatness and the triumph of our species. And this belief on stage must go from skepticism to possibility to probability before it is nipped off by whatever the modern word for fate is. And in hopelessness—George is able to rise to greatness—to kill his friend to save him. George is a hero and only heroes are worth writing about. *[LL*, pp. 562–63]

Lennie is not the only dreamer in the novel, however, and each of the other dreamers also seems afflicted with the loneliness of nonattainment. Most notable is the woman known only as "Curley's wife," a mere thing possessed by her flamboyant husband. From the start George recognizes the incipient danger posed by Curley's wife, a recognition that proves prophetically true: "'She's gonna make a mess. They's gonna be a bad mess about her. She's a jail bait all set on the trigger'" (p. 92). But Curley's wife is also caught in a hopeless little valley of small dreams. She dreamed of being an actress, of sweeping Hollywood, but when Curley came along he simply represented escape, and that was better than nothing. When Lennie shares his dream in response to her candor, she exclaims: "'You're nuts.... But you're a kinda nice fella. Jus' like a big baby. But a person can see kinda what you mean'" (p. 156). Similarly, Crooks, the stable hand and another small outcast, has his dream, one of companionship to assuage the terrible, haunting loneliness: "'Books ain't no good. A guy needs somebody—to be near him.... A guy goes nuts if he ain't got nobody'" (p. 127). And Candy too, another social outcast, is captivated by the dream: "'Sure they all want it. Everybody wants a little bit of land, not much. Jus' som'thin' that was his. Som'thin' he could live on and there couldn't nobody throw him off of it. I never had none'" (p. 133).

But through his careful foreshadowing Steinbeck suggests that each dream is doomed. Curley, the flamboyant fighter, stands ever ready to goad someone into a fight, particularly those larger than he, and who is larger on the ranch than Lennie? The dead mouse that Lennie strokes prefigures the dead girl's hair and the impossible dream of rabbits. And George knows these things; he senses the inevitable end. Early in the novel he tells Lennie to remember good hiding places, even as he tells him once more of the dream farm and the "fatta the lan'."

What keeps these little social outcasts going? What motivates them when all dreams seem doomed? In a sense the large-scale battle of *In Dubious Battle* is played out here in a small, quiet, but equally tragic scene, as if George and Lennie are the Everymen in a microcosmic universe. They are drawn together by the human need born of loneliness. George's words to Lennie, which form a dark refrain in the book, might have occurred equally well in *In Dubious Battle* or *The Grapes of Wrath*: "'Guys like us, that work on ranches, are the loneliest guys in the world. They got no family. They don't belong no place. They come to d ranch an' work up a stake and then they go into town and blow their stake, and the first thing you know they're poundin' their tail on some other ranch. They ain't got nothing to look ahead to'" (p. 28).

Even though the dream seems inevitably doomed, that is also at once man's glory—that he can dream and that others participate in the dream. Finally, this sets Lennie apart from the animal that he is imaged as being. At first the novel seems to set forth one more reductionistic pattern of imagery so familiar to Steinbeck's work. Lennie seems little more than an animal in human form: "Behind him walked his opposite, a huge man, shapeless of face, with large, pale eyes, and wide, sloping shoulders; and he walked heavily, dragging his feet a little, the way a bear drags his paws" (p. 9). Lennie bends to the water and drinks "with long gulps, snorting into the water like a horse" (p. 10). After drinking, he "dabbled his big paw in the water and wiggled his fingers so the water arose in little splashes" (p. 11). But as Tularecito rises above the animal by virtue of his creative gift, Lennie also rises above the animal in several ways. He is, for example, marked by kindness, a trait that at once sets him above Curley. Lennie is sensitive to the small and the forlorn, and it is no accident that Crooks and Curley's wife confide freely in him. But he does lack the rational acuity to survive in this society; killing Curley's wife is not qualitatively different for Lennie from killing the mouse. As Howard Levant points out, "The relative meaninglessness of his victims substitutes pathos for tragedy."[32] Clearly, Lennie is not a tragic figure, for he has nothing of the required nobility about him. But in a sense the deeper tragedy lies in his pathos; there is no place for a Lennie in society. Yet in the novel there is a kind of subtle reversal of animal imagery that makes animals of those who establish society's norms that disallow the survival of a Lennie. In the story of Tularecito, Miss Martin is closer to the animal in her fanatical insistence that Tularecito be whipped. In *Of Mice and Men*, Curley is closer to the animal in his predatory desire to fight. Oppression of any life is the animalistic trait, the struggle for survival that kills off or hides away the weaker members. For Steinbeck, on the other hand, that human life, which might be observable upon first glance as animalistic, often carries a warm dignity. While Lennie is a social misfit, it may be because society itself is ill.

Although *Of Mice and Men* quickly became one of Steinbeck's most popular works, it met with a great deal of puzzlement. Readers may have expected another angry *In Dubious Battle* from him and got instead this sad little drama of something that happened, something so small it escapes common attention. George walks away at the end just one more bindlestiff. Yet part of Steinbeck's success here lies in investing those small, barely noticeable lives with both pathos and dignity. If, as Carlson points out, there is a right way to kill a cripple, one still wonders why the cripple has to be killed.

But Steinbeck himself was dissatisfied with the novel, largely on aesthetic grounds. With the failed effort to block *In Dubious Battle* for the stage, he wanted very much to succeed with this effort. Steinbeck referred to the book as an experiment "designed to teach me to write for the theatre" (*LL*, p. 132), and he often spoke of it in perjorative terms such as a "simple little thing," or "the Mice book."[33] Whatever his attitude, the dramatic adaptation, like the novel, was a commercial success, opening at the Music Box Theatre in New York on November 23, 1937, and running for 207 performances.

Steinbeck at this time, however, was back home in California, well into the background work for his greatest achievement, *The Grapes of Wrath*.

**Notes**

30. Antonia Seixas, "John Steinbeck and the Non-Teleological Bus," in Tedlock and Wicker, eds., *Steinbeck and His Critics*, p. 277.

31. Peter Lisca, *The Wide World of John Steinbeck*, p. 135.

32. Howard Levant, *The Novels of John Steinbeck: A Critical Study*, p. 138.

33. Steinbeck presented his own theory of drama in a brief article in *Stage* (January, 1938), a theory discussed in its relation to *Of Mice and Men* by Howard Levant in *The Novels of John Steinbeck*, pp. 130–44.

## Lawrence William Jones on Why *Of Mice and Men* Is Not a Parable

*Tortilla Flat*, Steinbeck's first commercially successful novel, was also the first to employ the conventions of parable extensively and to discuss—albeit satirically—the subject or morality. Its most pervasive fabular element is again the inverted archetype as structural framework, in this case the story of King Arthur and his knights. Instead of seeking fame and fortune, Steinbeck's antiheroes consciously seek to preserve their anonymity while coping with the problems of subsistence living. Yet in their alignment against the dragon of civilized society, these paisanos have a code of values as rigid as that of the Round Table and comic rituals as ceremonious as those in *Morte d'Arthur*. This novel's formulable statement is essentially the triumph of human community over selfish individualism, with the community looking much like the group-man

Steinbeck was to introduce in his next novel. Pilon, aware of both his essential selfhood and his commitment to the group, is primarily the balanced man who stimulates the "knights" toward a strong sense of communal identity. About the only thing that keeps *Tortilla Flat* from becoming a parable of the type described above is its lack of serious moral purpose.

The next four novels, in which the critical consensus generally finds the best work Steinbeck ever produced, reveal a strong personal interest in the social issues of the thirties. For this major reason these novels lose many of the fabular elements which the first four had exhibited, but principally they lose the nature of being constructed to embody formulable statements in fictional terms, for the author is more intent upon accurate portrayals of current social dilemmas. *In Dubious Battle* contains the first explicit statement of Steinbeck's short-lived "group-man" hypothesis—which reappeared as a minor element in *The Grapes of Wrath* and was finally abandoned in *The Moon Is Down*. Mac, the communist strike-organizer becomes the group's "eye," and the workers under his direction form a unit to protect themselves against the powerful landowners. Yet Steinbeck does not advocate group-man; in fact he was adamant that there be "no author's moral point of view"[29] in the novel, that it merely give an objective (or non-teleological) presentation of the events and leave judgment to the reader. This novel's characters are at least vague harbingers of those seen repeatedly in the parables. Mac, Jim, London, and Doctor Burton are all something less than fully-rounded characters because they represent certain ideas and ideologies. They are not part of a controlling ethical pattern as in parable, but they work part-time as Steinbeck's spokesmen.

Although *The Red Pony* tends away from the major techniques of parable form, the Carl Tiflin–Billy Buck polarity presents, as in the later parables, Steinbeck's balanced man confronting an individual whose actions betray an insensitivity to the wholeness of life's texture. Under the provocation of his disciplinarian father and the warm tutelage of the ranch hand, young Jody gradually acquires an acceptance of death and suffering as intrinsic parts of life. Except for the satiric "St.

Katy the Virgin," a modified beast fable which shares the general character of the fabliaux the remaining stories in *The Long Valley* are cut from much the same cloth as *The Red Pony*. The fabular dimension of Steinbeck's first experiment with the hybrid form of play-novelette, *Of Mice and Men*, lies in the characterization of its protagonists. Lennie is a kind of American Everyman in his search for property and happiness, a dumb brute whose primeval loving nature somehow always ends up against the brutishness of mankind that continually but paradoxically triumphs over deep-set benevolence. George, who understands the nature of his relationship to Lennie, the need for their reassuring rituals, and even the necessity of shooting his friend, draws the reader to sympathize with Lennie's plight and to recognize the aura of fate that hangs over the events. But to have made *Of Mice and Men* a parable, Steinbeck would have had to infuse a moral lesson, which he did not do; and thus we experience the action rather than merely give it mental assent.

**Note**

29. Quoted by Lisca, *Wide World*, 114.

## MARILYN CHANDLER MCENTYRE ON CAIN, ABEL, AND INNOCENCE

Though not derived as directly from the story of Cain and Abel as *East of Eden*, and certainly not as ambitious as that novel in its attempts to explore the ramifications of the ancient tale, *Of Mice and Men* is still, in its way, a compelling invitation to revisit the biblical myth and recast its significance in new terms. The bevy of critics who have dismissed this small "play-novelette" as one of Steinbeck's lesser works if not failures, calling it exaggerated, mechanical, woodenly allegorical, and melodramatically parabolic, may have failed fully to appreciate the lasting power of allegory and parable even for the presumed audience of post-Freudian, post-Joycean readers.[1]

The apparent simplicity of this stark little tragedy (a term some think carries more weight than the tale can bear) belies the magnitude and complexity of the moral questions it raises. Roughly speaking, those questions are riddles of discernment: when is "evil" not really evil and "good" not really good? When do those "conditions which look alike" deceive us into false judgment? How do we know the good when it can look so like evil? Like the theologians and folklorists who transfer the logic of *"felix culpa"* to Eve's disobedience and proclaim it the first act of self-liberation, Steinbeck, along with a number of other modern writers, offers a revisionist perspective on Cain's story, attempting to understand this dark "hero" in terms of his willingness to accept the burden of consciousness, and ultimately the responsibility for murder in the effort to be his brother's keeper.

The situation of George, the "Cain" figure in this novel, is that of anyone limited by the dependencies of a weaker partner and wondering why the "virtue" of innocence seems so often to thrust moral and practical responsibility upon the one who consents to the fall into experience. Surely one of the questions the story raises is how much responsibility one can take for another human being. Getting the right relationship between independence, dependence, and interdependence has been a particularly vexed matter in American culture where the social contracts of family and friendship have been so variously and loosely construed, especially in marginal subcultures like that of the itinerant farm workers in this novel.

To recast Cain and Abel as George and Lennie, dispossessed survivors of an inequitable economic system, bound by a common vision of family life and shared labor, protector and protected and, humanly speaking, each other's *raison d'être*, is to clothe the old tale not only with poignancy and pathos but also with an audacious and uncomfortable immediacy. It is also to reframe our most basic hypotheses about that tale: What if Abel's gentleness were in fact weakness of mind or body? What if Cain's question to God could be read not as a rhetorical gesture of defiance, but as a cry of anguish wrung from a frustrated elder brother whose patience with the younger has been worn to the last thread? What if there are legitimate alternative readings to this moral tale? How shall we travel the forked path it maps?

In its framework of moral paradox, the story teaches us to reckon with the shadow. To empathize with Cain is to reevaluate what we call evil. To see the consequences of Lennie's "innocence" is to reconsider "things done ill, or done to others' harm / which once you took for exercise of virtue."[2] It is to complicate the idea of childlike innocence with a certain informed skepticism that says neither children nor those we call "innocents" are free of guile. Thus in the opening scene, when George catches Lennie with a dead mouse in his hand, Lennie makes "an elaborate pantomime of innocence," protesting transparently, "'What mouse, George? I ain't got no mouse.'" George replies coldly, "'You gonna give me that mouse or do I have to sock you?'"[3] The themes of innocence and violence are introduced and complicated here at one stroke. Lennie is indeed an "innocent," and also, like a child, manipulative and scheming in his own limited way. George's violence already has to be seen in the context of his taking responsibility, being the one to see the larger picture, to foresee consequences and to control Lennie's behavior for their mutual welfare.

Critics have attacked Steinbeck's relegation of the Abel role to a character who, being feeble-minded, cannot be assigned moral responsibility and so cannot bear the moral weight of his role in this drama of justice and mercy. This particular twist on the figure of the "innocent man," however, compels the reader to identify closely with the slayer of the innocent, to participate in his predicament, and to raise a troubling question about the economy of guilt: one man's innocence may require another man's guilt. To preserve innocence is costly, and finally undesirable. The fall requires humans to come into consciousness, and therefore into conscience, to experience guilt, and thereby be pointed toward redemption. Those who are willing to assume the moral responsibility of full participation in the muddy and ambiguous human condition, to be soiled and sinful, and to wrestle with intolerable ambiguities, emerge into a moral maturity unattainable by the "pure." The difference between becoming like a little child and remaining like one is vast. The first is an apotheosis of wisdom; the second either an infirmity or an abdication.

Purity is an old American theme, hardly peculiar to American culture, but certainly an abiding theme in literature and an axis of the moral reasoning that characterizes collective self-definition and public debate.[4] Every generation has needed its literary and political prophets to remind them that the pure in spirit may be blessed, but purists are dangerous, and a simplistic pursuit or valorization of purity is a kind of moral retardation, if not willful ignorance. When not willful—when it is, as in Lennie's case, an infirmity—it still exacts a cost; someone has to take on the burden of practical decision-making and planning that is required to carve out a place on earth to call home. And to do that, one must enter into compromising negotiation with world, flesh, and devil.

This was Cain's enterprise. A farmer and tiller of soil, whose name means "possession," he is indicted, among other things, for reducing the gifts of God to the terms of human economy, for presuming to own the land, and later for founding and investing his hope in the earthly city. The builders of the Tower of Babel are referred to as Cain's descendants—those who sought to secure and solidify their own base of power, literally to monumentalize it and fix it for all time, and by imperializing the territory between earth and heaven, to stake a final claim to the things of this earth and seek salvation in them rather than in the promises of their God.

This theme of presumption, brought into the twentieth century and placed in the framework of American capitalism, where private property is an index of success and independence, becomes both more personal and more problematic for modern readers. The Cain and Abel story is about a zero-sum economy, in which the success of one implies the diminishment or failure of the other. Thus the murder is predicated not only on an illegitimate seizure of power over life and death, but also on a radical reduction of divine economy to human terms. Rather than returning to God to understand the terms of acceptable sacrifice, and being willing to seek what would please Him, Cain seeks instead to eliminate the offense of comparison by eliminating the foil that defines him as a failure. For George to dream of "making a stake" so he and Lennie can have their "little place" hardly seems culpable, based though it is on the very notions of private property, possession, ownership, and exclusion that relate capitalism to the sin of Cain. But for Steinbeck to make explicit that relationship between capitalistic pursuit of self-interest and the original crime of murder is to hack at one of the thickest roots of American culture.

Post-industrial capitalism as a framework of social and therefore moral life has forced society to reassess the terms in which it thinks about sin, guilt, and goodness. The erosion of family ties and therefore of the old tribal ethics of filial piety and fraternal loyalty has made the social contract more ambiguous. It is less clear now than it once was in what way we are our brothers' keepers, who, indeed, are our "brothers," what we may expect to give and receive, what are the terms of communal life, and how to do good in a system whose evils continue to implicate us all in erosion of intimate life, secularization of social life, and loss of moral direction.

One of the deepest motives in great literature of all ages, and in a particular way in modern literature since Faust's Mephistopheles and Byron's brooding heroes, has been to seek ways to reframe moral questions that move us beyond simplistic application of the categories of good and evil into a larger awareness of how, in human life and the human psyche, good and evil are deeply and interdependently entangled—how we live in a realm where blacks and whites turn grey.

The Cain and Abel story provides a useful vehicle for this kind of moral reassessment, precisely because it is predicated on strong dualities and polarities. Polarities, carefully considered, lead us to paradox. Extremes of any human attribute tend to point to and often generate their opposites. So Steinbeck, among numerous other nineteenth- and twentieth-century novelists and playwrights, returned to that story as an appropriate paradigm for examining the moral complexities of the time. His experiments with the Cain–Abel motif invite readers to consider how opposites may be related, and how "conditions that look alike" may contradict themselves. In Lennie, the half-wit, we have to consider the relationship between innocence and vacuity; in George, his protector and murderer, between cruelty and kindness. In the obvious and extreme oppositions between them we are finally led to contemplate what is the bond that unites them and, indeed, in what sense they are not simply opposites but also doubles, whose deep similarities belie their differences. Superficially, the differences are archetypal:

> The first man was small and quick, dark of face, with restless eyes and sharp, strong features. Every part of him was defined: small, strong hands, slender arms, a thin and bony nose. Behind him walked his opposite, a huge man, shapeless of face, with large, pale eyes, with wide, sloping shoulders; and he walked heavily, dragging his feet a little, the way a bear drags his paws. His arms did not swing at his sides, but hung loosely. (2)

The sharp physical differences: small and dark, big and fair, sharp human intelligence posed against animal-like dumbness—suggest larger contrasts: dark and light, aggression and submission, movement and stasis, and finally life and death.

Indeed, Lennie costs George a great deal in life energy. George experiences his caretaking of Lennie as a sysyphean task: "I ain't got nothing to do. Might jus' as well spen' al my time tellin' you things and then you forget 'em, and I tell you again" (4). He is controller, instructor, protector. He carries Lennie's work card and bus ticket for him, undertakes to foresee the trouble he might cause and prevent it, commits himself to second-guessing Lennie's purposes and behavior as watchful parents do recalcitrant children. George talks; Lennie acts. George has to engage in careful manipulation to secure the field of action in which he can act—to get them hired so the boss can see Lennie work. Once that is done, Lennie may be proven to be the better worker. "You jus' stand there and don't say nothing" George tells his charge. "If he finds out what a crazy bastard you are, we won't get no job, but if he sees ya work before he hears ya talk, we're set. Ya got that?" (6)

Thus the theme of the "acceptable sacrifice" is refocused in such a way as to lead us to consider the sacrifice or contribution required of one partner to enable the work of the other to receive due regard. George's reiteration to the boss that Lennie is the better worker, weak of mind, but exceptionally capable of performing the work he's being hired to do, directs the boss's attention to the goodness of the offering and prevents Lennie from being judged in the wrong terms. Consequently the weaker brother has the means to please the "father" even though the gifts of the stronger, which ultimately seem to count for little, are necessary to the welfare of the weaker.

**Notes**

1. See, for instance, Howard Levant, *The Novels of John Steinbeck: A Critical Study* (Columbia, MO: University of Missouri Press, 1974, 133–144).

2. T.S. Eliot, "Little Gidding" in *Four Quartets*, included in *T.S. Eliot: The Complete Poems and Plays 1909–1950* (New York: Harcourt, Brace & World, Inc.), 142.

3. John Steinbeck, *Of Mice and Men* (NY: Bantam Books, 1937, 1965), 9. All further references to this work will be found in the text.

4. For a useful discussion of the idea of "purity" in American politics and public discourse, see Garry Wills' *Under God* (NY: Touchstone Press, 1990), relevant here to an understanding of the particularly "American" character of Steinbeck's moral universe.

## WILLIAM GOLDHURST ON THE NOVEL'S VISION

The title of the story has a twofold application and significance. First it refers to naturalistic details within the texture of the novella: Lennie likes to catch mice and stroke their fur with his fingers. This is a particularly important point for two reasons: it establishes Lennie's fatal weakness for stroking soft things and, since he invariably kills the mice he is petting, it foreshadows his deadly encounter with Curley's wife. Second, the title is, of course, a fragment from the poem by Robert Burns, which gives emphasis to the idea of the futility of human endeavor or the vanity of human wishes. "The best laid schemes o' mice and men / Gang aft a-gley / An' leave us nought but grief an' pain / For promised joy." This notion is obviously of major importance in the novella, and it may be said to be Steinbeck's main theme on the surface level of action and development of character.

(...)

This is Steinbeck's portrait of Cain in the modern world, or Man Alone, whose fate is so severe that he may feel compelled to echo the words of Cain to the Lord: "My punishment is more than I can bear." In *Of Mice and Men* Steinbeck gives us the case history of two simple mortals who try to escape the homelessness, economic futility, and psychological soul corruption that Scripture embodies in the curse of Cain.

If in scene 1 Lennie and George affirm their fraternity openly and without embarrassment, in scene 2 George is more hesitant. "He's my ... cousin," he tells the ranch boss. "I told his old lady I'd take care of him." This is no betrayal on George's part, but a cover-up required by the circumstances. For the boss is highly suspicious of the Lennie–George fellowship "You takin' his pay away from him?" he asks George. "I never seen one guy take so much trouble for another guy." A short time later Curley also sounds the note of suspicion, extending it by a particularly nasty innuendo: when George says, "We travel together," Curley replies, "Oh, so it's that way." Steinbeck is implying here the general response of most men toward seeing two individuals who buddy around together in a friendless world where isolation is the order of the day: there must be exploitation involved, either financial or sexual. At the same time Steinbeck is developing the allegorical level of his story by suggesting that the attitude of Cain ("I know not: Am I my brother's keeper?") has become universal.[3] Even the sympathetic and understanding Slim expresses some wonder at the Lennie–George fraternity. "Ain't many guys travel around together," Slim says in scene 2. "I don't know why. Maybe ever'body in the whole damned world is scared of each other." This too, as Steinbeck interprets the biblical story, is a part of Cain's curse: distrust. Later on, in order to give the theme of Aloneness another dimension, Steinbeck stresses the solitude of Crooks and Curley's wife, both of whom express a craving for company and "someone to talk to."

Notwithstanding the fact that they are obviously swimming against the current, Lennie and George continue to reaffirm their solidarity all along, right up to and including the last moments of Lennie's life in scene 6. Here a big rabbit, which Lennie in his disturbed state of mind has hallucinated, tells the half-wit fugitive that George is sick of him and is going to go away and leave him. "He won't!" Lennie cries. "He won't do nothing like that. I know George. Me an' him travels together." Actually Steinbeck's novella advances and develops, ebbs and flows, around the basic image of the Lennie–George relationship. Almost all the characters react to it in one way or another as the successive scenes unfold. In scenes 1, 2, and 3, despite the discouraging opinions of outsiders, the companionship remains intact and unthreatened. Midway into scene 3 the partnership undergoes augmentation when Candy is admitted into the scheme to buy the little farm. Late in scene 4 Crooks offers himself as another candidate for the fellowship of soul brothers and dreamers. This is the high point of optimism as regards the main theme of the story; this is the moment when a possible reversal of the curse of Cain seems most likely, as Steinbeck suggests that the answer to the Lord's question might be, "Yes, I am my brother's keeper." If we arrive at this point with any comprehension of the author's purposes, we find ourselves brought up short by the idea: what if this George–Lennie–Candy–Crooks fraternity were to become universal?

But later in the same scene, the entrance of Curley's wife signals the turning point as the prospects for the idea of brotherhood-as-a-reality begin to fade and darken. As throughout the story, she represents a force that destroys men and at the same time invites men to destroy her, as she will finally in scene 5 offer herself as a temptation which Lennie cannot resist, so in scene 4 Curley's wife sows the seeds that eventually disrupt the fellowship. Entering into the discussion in Crooks's room in the stable, she insults Crooks, Candy, and Lennie, laughs at their dream farm, and threatens to invent the kind of accusation that will get Crooks lynched.[4] Crooks, reminded of his position of impotence in a white man's society, immediately withdraws his offer to participate in the George–Lennie–Candy farming enterprise. But Crooks's withdrawal, while extremely effective as social criticism, is much more. It represents an answer to the question Steinbeck is considering all along: Is man meant to make his way alone or accompanied? Obviously this is one occasion, among many others in the story, when Steinbeck suggests the answer. Crooks's hope for fraternal living is short-lived. At the conclusion of the scene he sinks back into his Aloneness.

From this point on, even though the dream of fellowship on the farm remains active, the real prospects for its fulfillment decline drastically. In scene 5, after George and Candy discover the lifeless body of Curley's wife, they both face the realization that the little farm is now unattainable and the partnership dissolved. Actually the plan was doomed to failure from the beginning; for fraternal living cannot long survive in a world dominated by the Aloneness, homelessness, and economic futility which Steinbeck presents as the modern counterpart of Cain's curse. Immediately following his discovery of Curley's wife's body, George delivers a speech that dwells on the worst possible aftermath of Lennie's misdeed; and this is not the wrath of Curley or the immolation of Lennie or the loss of the farm, but the prospect of George's becoming a Man Alone; homeless, like all the others and a victim as well of economic futility: "I'll work my month an' I'll take my fifty bucks and I'll stay all night in some lousy cat house. Or I'll set in some poolroom til ever'body goes home. An' then I'll come back an' work another month an' I'll have fifty bucks more." This speech represents the true climax of the novella, for it answers the question that is Steinbeck's main interest throughout. Now we know the outcome of the Lennie–George experiment in fellowship, as we know the Aloneness of man's essential nature. In subtle ways, of course, Steinbeck has been hinting at this conclusion all along, as, for example, in the seven references spaced throughout scenes 2 and 3 to George's playing solitaire in the bunkhouse. For that matter the answer is implied in the very first line of the story when the author establishes his setting "a few miles south of Soledad ..." Soledad being at one and the same time a town in central California and the Spanish word for solitude, or aloneness. But there are still other suggested meanings inherent in the dream farm and the failure of the dream. The plan is doomed not only because human fellowship cannot survive in the post-Cain world, but also because the image of the farm, as conceived by George and Lennie and Candy, is overly idealized, the probability being that life, even if they obtained the farm, would not consist of the comfort, plenty, and inter-personal harmony they envision. The fruits and vegetables in abundance, the livestock and domestic animals, and the community of people involved ("Ain't gonna be no more trouble. Nobody gonna hurt nobody nor steal from 'em")—these are impractical expectations. George and Lennie, who were to some extent inspired by questions growing out of the story of Cain in chapter 4 of Genesis, want to retreat to chapter 2 and live in Eden! Of all ambitions in a fallen world, this is possibly the most unattainable; for paradise is lost, as the name of Steinbeck's hero, George Milton, suggests. And though there will always be men like Candy, who represents "sweet hope," the view of Crooks, who represents "black despair," is probably a more accurate appraisal of the human condition; "Nobody never gets to heaven, and nobody gets no land. It's just in their head. They're all the time talkin' about it, but it's just in their head." Obviously in this context Crooks's comment about nobody ever getting land refers not to literal ownership but to the dream of contentment entertained by the simple workmen who come and go on the ranch.

To pursue the Milton parallel a step further, we perceive immediately that Steinbeck has no intention of justifying the ways of God to man. On the contrary, if anything, *Of Mice and*

*Men* implies a critique of Hebrew-Christian morality, particularly in the area of the concept of punishment for sin. This opens up still another dimension of meaning in our interpretation of Steinbeck's novella. If George and Lennie fail to attain their dream farm (for reasons already explored), and the dream farm is a metaphor or image for heaven (as suggested by Crooks's speech in scene 4) then the failure to achieve the dream farm is most likely associated with the question of man's failure to attain heaven. Steinbeck's consideration of this last-named theme is not hard to find. Along this particular line of thought, Lennie represents one essential aspect of man—the animal appetites, the craving to touch and feel, the impulse toward immediate gratification of sensual desires.[5] George is the element of Reason which tries to control the appetites or, better still, to elevate them to a higher and more sublime level. As Lennie's hallucinatory rabbit advises him near the conclusion: "Christ knows George done ever'thing he could to jack you outa the sewer, but it don't do no good." Steinbeck suggests throughout that the appetites and Reason coexist to compose the nature of man. ("Me an' him travels together.") He goes on to suggest that the effort to refine man into something rare, saintly, and inhuman is another unattainable ambition. Even when Reason (George) manages to communicate to the appetites (Lennie) its urgent message ("You crazy son-of-a-bitch. You keep me in hot water all the time ... I never get no peace") the appetites are incapable of satisfying Reason's demands. This submerged thesis is suggested when Aunt Clara—like the big rabbit a product of Lennie's disturbed imagination—scolds Lennie in scene 6:

> "I tol' you an' tol' you. I tol' you. 'Min' George because he's such a nice fella an' good to you.' But you don't never take no care. You do bad things."
> And Lennie answered her, "I tried, Aunt Clara, ma'am. I tried and tried. I couldn' help it."[6]

The animal appetites, even though well attended and well intentioned, cannot be completely suppressed or controlled.

Thus, the best man can hope for is a kind of insecure balance of power between these two elements—which is, in fact, what most of the ranch hands accomplish, indulging their craving for sensual pleasure in a legal and commonplace manner each payday. Failing this, man must suppress absolutely the appetites that refuse to be controlled, as George does in the symbolic killing of Lennie at the conclusion of the novella. Possibly this is a veiled reference to the drastic mutilation of man's nature required by the Christian ethic. At the same time the theological implications of *Of Mice and Men* project the very highest regard for the noble experiment in fraternal living practiced by George and Lennie; and possibly the time scheme of their stay on the ranch—from Friday to Sunday—is a veiled reference to the sacrifice of Christ. He too tried to reverse the irreversible tide of Cain's curse by serving as the ultimate example of human brotherhood.

## Notes

3. One of Steinbeck's critics unconsciously confirms this discouraging thesis when he says, "Steinbeck represents George as being closely attached to Lennie. But George's feeling is not convincing because it is not that of most men in real life" (Woodburn O. Ross in Tedlock and Wicker, 175). To Mr. Ross we might reply, with John Steinbeck, *tant pis!* This is the same outlook that provides the context for the *tragedy* of George and Lennie!

4. First appearance suggests that Steinbeck might be guilty of antifeminist sentiment by his use of the Hemigwayesque "Men Without Women" theme: "Everything was fine with us boys until that trouble-making female came along," etc. Curley's wife, however, is represented as the victim of the same impulses as the men in the story; she too is impelled out of loneliness to seek company, *and* she too is the victim of a dream: "Coulda been in the movies, and had nice clothes," etc. With this emphasis Steinbeck includes Curley's wife in the problems and striving of all men who inherit the curse of Cain. In any case, though she does in fact have trouble-making propensities, she is no worse in this respect than her husband and overall is unquestionably a more sympathetic character than Curley.

5. Obviously Steinbeck faced a problem in his portrait of Lennie as a sympathetic though dangerous moron who has great difficulty in keeping his hands off women. (Compare William Faulkner's treatment of Benjy in *The Sound and the Fury*.) The author's entire

emphasis would have been thrown off balance if Lennie had attacked Curley's wife (or the girl in Weed) in some gross and lascivious manner. Clearly, if he were prone to this sort of behavior George would not be traveling with him in the first place. Lennie must be as he is—powerful and potentially dangerous, but essentially childlike and innocent for other reasons as well. His condition lends emphasis to the basic idea of general aloneness of men; if Lennie were normally intelligent, he would most likely be busy pursuing his own interests. Finally, the basic innocence of Lennie's sensual impulses reinforces Steinbeck's critique-of-Hebrew-Christian-morality theme by making the point that there is nothing evil, per se, in man's natural sensuality.

6. All my quotations from *Of Mice and Men* are taken from *The Portable Steinbeck*, Selected by Pascal Covici (New York: Viking Press, 1960), 227–323.

# Works by John Steinbeck

*Cup of Gold*, 1929.
*The Pastures of Heaven*, 1932.
*To a God Unknown*, 1933.
*Tortilla Flat*, 1935.
*In Dubious Battle*, 1936.
*Of Mice and Men*, 1937.
*Of Mice and Men: A Play in Three Acts*, 1937.
*The Red Pony*, 1937.
*The Long Valley*, 1938.
*The Grapes of Wrath*, 1939.
*The Forgotten Village*, 1941.
*Sea of Cortez*, 1941.
*Bombs Away*, 1942.
*The Moon is Down*, 1942.
*Cannery Row*, 1945.
*The Pearl*, 1947.
*The Wayward Bus*, 1947.
*A Russian Journal*, 1948.
*Burning Bright*, 1950.
*East of Eden*, 1952.
*Sweet Thursday*, 1954.
*The Short Reign of Pippin IV*, 1957.
*Once There Was a War*, 1958.
*The Winter of Our Discontent*, 1960.
*Travels with Charley in Search of America*, 1962.
*America and Americans*, 1966.
*The Acts of King Arthur and His Noble Knights*, posthumous,
    1976.

Annotated Bibliography

Benson, Jackson T. *The Short Novels of John Steinbeck: Critical Essays with a Checklist to Steinbeck Criticism.* Durham: Duke University Press, 1990.

A comparative study of Steinbeck's short novels, this work pays attention to the author's craft, characters, themes, and attendant strengths and weaknesses across several works.

Benson, Jackson T. *The True Adventures of John Steinbeck, Writer.* New York: Viking, 1984.

Regarded as the most authoritative biography available on the author. A more recent version, by Jay Parini, has more critical content, but Benson's covers well the details of the author's life and work.

French, Warren. *John Steinbeck's Fiction Revisited.* New York: Twayne Publishers, 1994.

Warren French's critical career started when he mounted an apparent defense of critics dismissing Steinbeck as a political propagandist. In later years, his work on Steinbeck's craft as a novelist, particularly his experimentation in structure and character, as well as the development of his theories on behavior, characterized what has become very valuable criticism.

Hadella, Charlotte. *Of Mice and Men: A Kinship of Powerlessness.* New York: Twayne Publishers, 1995.

One of the few book-length studies of the novel, Hadella's work draws on ideas of many critics (French, Owens, Levant) to provide a convincing reading about Steinbeck's philosophy.

Marsden, John L. "California Dreamin': The Significance of 'A Coupla Acres' in Steinbeck's *Of Mice and Men.*" *Western American Literature* 29:4 (Feb. 1995): pp. 291-297.

Considers the character of Lennie within Foucault's power theories.

Owens, Louis. *John Steinbeck's Re-Vision of America*. Athens: University of Georgia Press, 1985.

A frequently cited book in Steinbeck scholarship, this volume discusses *Of Mice and Men* a great deal, and does so in comparison to many of Steinbeck's major novels.

Steinbeck, Elaine, and Robert Wallsten. *Steinbeck: A Life in Letters*. London: Pan Books, 1979.

Steinbeck wrote thousands of letters over his lifetime, and often would write several in a single day. This collection provides useful insight into the author's attitudes, struggles, aesthetic and craft decisions, and the influence of others' opinions on his work. Many references are included about *Of Mice and Men*.

St. Pierre, Brian. *John Steinbeck: The California Years*. The Literary West Series. San Francisco: Chronicle Books, 1983.

This book tracks the sources for the many works Steinbeck set in California.

Timmerman, John H. *John Steinbeck's Fiction: The Aesthetics of the Road Taken*. Norman: University of Oklahoma Press, 1986.

A thorough examination of Steinbeck's technique and themes with significant attention paid to *Of Mice and Men*.

# Contributors

**Harold Bloom** is Sterling Professor of the Humanities at Yale University. He is the author of 30 books, including *Shelley's Mythmaking* (1959), *The Visionary Company* (1961), *Blake's Apocalypse* (1963), *Yeats* (1970), *A Map of Misreading* (1975), *Kabbalah and Criticism* (1975), *Agon: Toward a Theory of Revisionism* (1982), *The American Religion* (1992), *The Western Canon* (1994), and *Omens of Millennium: The Gnosis of Angels, Dreams, and Resurrection* (1996). *The Anxiety of Influence* (1973) sets forth Professor Bloom's provocative theory of the literary relationships between the great writers and their predecessors. His most recent books include *Shakespeare: The Invention of the Human* (1998), a 1998 National Book Award finalist, *How to Read and Why* (2000), *Genius: A Mosaic of One Hundred Exemplary Creative Minds* (2002), *Hamlet: Poem Unlimited* (2003), *Where Shall Wisdom Be Found?* (2004), and *Jesus and Yahweh: The Names Divine* (2005). In 1999, Professor Bloom received the prestigious American Academy of Arts and Letters Gold Medal for Criticism. He has also received the International Prize of Catalonia, the Alfonso Reyes Prize of Mexico, and the Hans Christian Andersen Bicentennial Prize of Denmark.

**Gabriel Welsch**'s short stories, poems, and reviews have appeared in *Georgia Review*, *Mid-American Review*, *Crab Orchard Review*, and *Cream City Review*. He regularly reviews literature for *Harvard Review*, *Missouri Review*, *Slope*, and *Small Press Review*. He received a Pennsylvania Council on the Arts Fellowship for Literature in fiction in 2003.

**Charlotte Cook Hadella** is a Professor in the Department of English and Writing at Southern Oregon University in Ashland. She is the author of *Of Mice and Men: A Kinship of Powerlessness* and *Warm Springs Millennium: Voices from the Reservation*.

**Peter Lisca** was a Fulbright Scholar and Professor Emeritus of English at the University of Florida and the author of *The Wide World of John Steinbeck* and other books.

**Warren French** is Professor Emeritus of English at Indiana University and the author of numerous books, including a half-dozen books on Steinbeck's work alone.

**John Seelye** is a Graduate Research Professor of American Literature at the University of Florida in Gainesville and is the general editor of the Penguin American Classics editions. He is the author of numerous critical books.

**Louis Owens** was Professor of English and Native American Studies and Director of Creative Writing at the University of California, Davis. The author of numerous books of criticism and essays, as well as of several short stories, he published two books on Steinbeck.

**Howard Levant** taught at Hartwick College and Pepperdine University. Among his publications are *The Novels of John Steinbeck* and *The Writer and the World*.

**John H. Timmerman** is Professor of English at Calvin College. He is the author of numerous critical works, including *John Steinbeck's Fiction: The Aesthetics of the Road Taken* and *The Dramatic Landscape of Steinbeck's Short Stories*.

**Lawrence William Jones**, author of *John Steinbeck as Fabulist*, was a Research Student in the Department of English at the University of Leicester.

**Marilyn Chandler McEntyre** is Associate Professor of Literature at Westmont College in Santa Barbara California. She is the author of two books of poetry, *In Quiet Light: Poems on Vermeer's Women* and *Drawn to the Light: Poems on Rembrandt's Religious Paintings*.

**William Goldhurst** is Professor Emeritus of English and Humanities at the University of Florida. He is the author of *F. Scott Fitzgerald and His Contemporaries*, among other works.

# Acknowledgments

*Of Mice and Men: A Kinship of Powerlessness* by Charlotte Cook Hadella. New York: Twayne Publishers (1995): 4–7; 27–32. © 1995 Twayne Publishers. Reprinted by permission of the Gale Group.

*The Wide World of John Steinbeck* by Peter Lisca. New Brunswick: Rutgers University Press (1958): 134–140. © 1958 Rutgers University Press. Reprinted by permission.

*John Steinbeck* by Warren French. New York: Twayne Publishers (1961): 73–76. *John Steinbeck* Second Edition, Revised. Boston: Twayne Publishers (1975): 87–91. © 1975 Twayne Publishers. Reprinted by permission of the Gale Group.

"Come Back to the Boxcar, Leslie Honey: Or, Don't Cry For Me Madonna, Just Pass the Milk: Steinbeck and Sentimentality," by John Seelye. From *Beyond Boundaries: Rereading John* Steinbeck, ed. Susan Shillinglaw and Kevin Hearle. Tuscaloosa: The University of Alabama Press (2002): 25–27. © 2002 The University of Alabama Press. Reprinted by permission.

*John Steinbeck's Re-Vision of America* by Louis Owens. Athens: The University of Georgia Press (1985): 102–106. © 1985 The University of Georgia Press. Reprinted by permission.

*The Novels of John Steinbeck: A Critical Study* by Howard Levant. Columbia: University of Missouri Press (1974): 133–144. © 1974 University of Missouri Press. Reprinted by permission.

*John Steinbeck's Fiction Revisited* by warren French. New York: Twayne Publishers (1994): 73–74. © Twayne Publishers. Reprinted by permission of the Gale Group.

*John Steinbeck's Fiction: The Aesthetics of the Road Taken* by John H. Timmerman. Norman: University of Oklahoma Press (1986): 96–101. © 1986 University of Oklahoma Press. Reprinted by permission.

"John Steinbeck as Fabulist," by Lawrence William Jones. From *The Betrayal of Brotherhood in the Work of John Steinbeck*, ed. Michael J. Meyer. Lewiston: The Edwin Mellen Press (2000): 70–72. © 2000 The Edwin Mellen Press. Reprinted by permission.

"*Of Mice and Men*: A Story of Innocence Retained," by Marilyn Chandler McEntyre. From *The Betrayal of Brotherhood in the Work of John Steinbeck*, ed. Michael J. Meyer. Lewiston: The Edwin Mellen Press (2000): 203–209. © 2000 The Edwin Mellen Press. Reprinted by permission.

"*Of Mice and Men*: John Steinbeck's Parable of the Curse of Cain," by William Goldhurst. From *The Betrayal of Brotherhood in the Work of John Steinbeck*, ed. Michael J. Meyer. Lewiston: The Edwin Mellen Press (2000): 225–235. © 2000 The Edwin Mellen Press. Reprinted by permission.

Every effort has been made to contact the owners of copyrighted material and secure copyright permission. Articles appearing in this volume generally appear much as they did in their original publication with few or no editorial changes. Those interested in locating the original source will find bibliographic information in the bibliography and acknowledgments sections of this volume.

# Index

Characters in literary works are indexed by first name (if any), followed by the name of the work in parentheses

**A**

*Acts of King Arthur and His Noble Knights* (Steinbeck), 12
American Dream theme
  in *The Grapes of Wrath*, 88
  in *Of Mice and Men*, 7, 13, 15–16, 21–24, 27–29, 37–39, 42, 45, 47–51, 53–55, 57, 60, 62, 67, 70, 72–73, 75–88, 96–98, 100–1, 103–5, 112, 117–20
*American Tragedy, An* (Dreiser), 8

**B**

Baker, Carlos, 73
Beach, Joseph Warren, 72
*Bitter Harvest: A History of California Farm workers, 1870–1941* (Daniel), 62
*Bombs Away* (Steinbeck), 11
Burns, Robert, 73, 76, 82–84, 116
Burgess, Anthony, 7
Burroughs, Edgar Rice, 83

**C**

Candy (*Of Mice and Men*), 40, 44, 46, 52, 64, 81, 87
  and his dog, 17, 27, 31, 34–37, 39, 54–55, 66–67, 70, 94, 96, 105
  and the dream, 15–16, 38–39, 42, 45, 47–48, 55, 71, 80, 85, 97, 104, 117–19
  and solitude, 25–26, 91
*Cannery Row* (Steinbeck), 10–11, 86
Carlson (*Of Mice and Men*), 53
  brute, 16, 30–31, 34, 37, 40, 55, 58, 65, 91, 101, 106

death of Candy's dog, 17, 35–36, 39, 54, 66–67, 87, 94, 96–97, 105
Companionship theme
  in *Of Mice and Men*, 8, 43–45, 48, 72, 79–80, 85, 104, 116–19, 121
Crane, Stephen, 76
Crooks, the Stable Buck (*Of Mice and Men*), 36, 47, 55–56, 81
  and companionship, 43–45, 48, 48, 72, 79–80, 85, 104, 117–19
  description of, 41–42, 67, 91, 106
  injuries, 15, 25, 42, 45
  memories, 45
  pessimism of, 100–1
  rejection and isolation of, 17, 25–26, 41, 43, 97, 117–19
*Cup of Gold* (Steinbeck), 10, 77
Curley (*Of Mice and Men*), 39, 49–50, 58, 66, 75, 116
  confrontation with Lennie, 17, 27–29, 40–41, 46–48, 54, 67–68, 70, 76, 80–81, 97, 105
  description of, 31, 54, 65, 91
  hot-headedness, 15, 26, 52–55, 81, 92, 93–94, 100–1, 106
Curley's wife (*Of Mice and Men*), 28, 33, 37, 101, 117
  death of, 17, 48, 51–53, 68, 74–75, 81, 86, 91, 92, 93, 98, 106, 115, 118
  dreams of, 49–50, 81, 104
  fear and hatred of husband, 46, 50, 92

physical presence, 15, 65, 70, 72, 74, 80, 83, 85, 117
red, 15, 29, 49
seduction of Lennie, 17, 42–43, 47, 49–51, 67, 92–94, 97, 118
and Slim, 36, 40

**D**

Daniel, Cletus E., 62
*Death of a Salesman* (Miller), 77
Death theme
American, 59
in *Of Mice and Men*, 31, 48–55
Dreiser, Theodore, 8

**E**

*East of Eden* (Steinbeck), 11–12, 103, 109
Eden metaphors
in *Of Mice and Men*, 23, 83, 86–87, 119

**F**

Farrell, James, 83
Faulkner, William, 8
"Fingers of Cloud" (Steinbeck), 60
Fitzgerald, F. Scott, 13
*Forgotten Village, The* (Steinbeck), 11
Frost, Robert, 82

**G**

George Milton (*Of Mice and Men*), 30, 35, 43–44, 52, 66
care of Lennie, 7–8, 15, 19–20, 23, 26–29, 31–32, 34, 36, 38, 40, 42, 48–49, 53, 55–56, 58, 65, 74, 76–77, 79, 87, 90, 93–94, 109–11, 114–15
description of, 18, 25, 27–28, 33, 63–64
dream of, 7, 15–16, 21–23, 27–29, 38–39, 42, 45, 47–48, 51, 53–55, 57, 67, 70–73,

75–88, 96–98, 100–1, 103–5, 112, 117, 119–20
execution of Lennie, 8, 18, 28, 39, 53, 57–58, 68, 71, 76–78, 81, 86–88, 92, 95–96, 98, 104, 114, 121
itinerant worker, 13
morals of, 20, 33, 36–37, 91, 95
storytelling of, 21–22, 38–39, 53, 57, 70–71, 80, 96
threats of, 17, 28
trust of Slim, 33–34, 41, 53–54, 57–58, 78
tumultuous past of, 19, 69, 80, 102, 116
*Grapes of Wrath, The* (Steinbeck), 11, 61, 101
biblical style of, 7
dream theme in, 88
movie, 11
setting of, 69, 103
social force of, 8
success of, 79, 83, 107–8

**H**

Harte, Bret, 83
Hemingway, Ernest, 8, 72

**I**

Imagery in *Of Mice and Men*
animal, 25, 85, 105–6, 117, 120
color, 15, 18, 29, 49
Eden, 23
innocent and the cruel, 31
snake and evil, 24, 55
*In Dubious Battle* (Steinbeck), 11, 17, 61, 75, 96
mob and leaders in, 73, 79, 108
criticism, 13, 100–1
setting of, 69, 106

**K**

Kaufman, George S., 79
Kazan, Elia, 12

**L**

Lennie (*Of Mice and Men*), 30, 43, 46, 66
   childlike, 7, 15, 19–20, 25, 32–35, 42, 74, 80, 85–86, 90–91, 101, 109–12, 114–15
   confrontation with Curley, 17, 40–41, 46–48, 67–68, 70, 76, 80–81, 97, 105
   death of, 8, 18, 28, 39, 52–55, 57–58, 68, 71, 76–78, 81, 86–88, 91–92, 95–96, 98–99, 104, 114
   death of animals, 19, 48–49, 67–68, 70, 80, 84, 86–87, 93, 105, 111, 115
   and the death of Curley's wife, 17, 48, 51–53, 68, 74, 81, 86, 91–94, 98, 106, 115, 118, 121
   description of, 18, 31
   and the dream, 15–16, 21–24, 27–29, 37–38, 42, 45, 47–48, 50–51, 53–54, 57, 67, 70–73, 79–80, 83–88, 96–98, 103–5, 112, 117–20
   escape of, 52–53, 81, 116
   humanity of, 25
   itinerant worker, 13
   strength of, 26, 63–65, 70, 80, 90, 115
   temptations of, 17, 29
   threats of, 17, 28
   trouble and sorrow of, 7, 15, 23–24, 27, 29, 36, 39–40, 42, 44, 49, 53, 56, 66–67
   tumultuous past of, 19, 69–70, 80, 86, 102
   violence and fears of, 7–8, 38–39, 48–49, 51, 53, 55–57, 67–68, 86, 92, 94, 97, 111
*Long Valley, The* (Steinbeck), 109

**M**

Miller, Arthur, 77

*Moon Is Down, The* (Steinbeck), 11, 108
Moore, Harry Thornton, 89
Morality and consequence themes, 10, 12
"Murder" (Steinbeck), 63

**O**

*Of Mice and Men* (Steinbeck), 11
   Arthurian influence on, 74–78
   Cain and Abel story in, 24, 53, 84–85, 87–88, 109–19, 121
   character lists, 15–16
   counterinfluence in, 8
   critical views, 7–8, 59–122
   dramatic values in, 8
   economic intensity of, 7
   metaphors in, 23, 25
   movie and stage production, 14, 73, 78–79, 88–89, 92, 107
   narrative, 14, 18, 26, 41, 49, 51–52, 66, 68, 78
   philosophies of, 78–82
   play-novelette, 14, 17, 63–69, 88–99, 106, 109, 115–17, 120–21
   political influences on, 59–63
   sentimentality of, 7, 33
   story behind, 13–14
   structure of, 17, 89–90, 96
   success of, 11, 14, 78, 83
   summary and analysis, 17–58
   vision of, 115–22
*Once There Was a War* (Steinbeck), 12
O'Neill, Eugene, 7–8
"Open Boat, The" (Crane), 76
*Our Town* (Wilder), 14, 79

**P**

*Pastures of Heaven, The* (Steinbeck), 86, 98
*Pearl, The* (Steinbeck), 11, 69

**R**

"Raid, The" (Steinbeck), 61
*Red Pony, The* (Steinbeck), 11, 14, 82, 87
setting of, 105, 108–9
Ricketts, Ed, 10, 78

**S**

Salinas, California, 75
Steinbeck's birthplace, 9–10, 12–13, 59
*Sea of Cortez, The* (Steinbeck), 11, 73
Setting of *Of Mice and Men*, 104–7
barn, 48, 67–68
bunkhouse, 24–25, 28, 31–37, 39, 41, 64, 66–67, 69, 75, 80, 90
Crook's room, 41, 67
Salinas River grove, 18, 24, 55–57, 63–65, 68–70, 79, 91, 102–
*Sister Carrie* (Dreiser), 8
Slim (*Of Mice and Men*), 41–42, 45, 51, 66–67
and Curley's wife, 36, 40
description of, 29–30, 65, 91, 100
leader of the bunkhouse, 16, 30, 34–36, 39, 41, 53–54, 80–81
recognition of dignity, 8, 30–33, 57–58, 65, 77–78, 81–82, 85–86, 88, 95, 116–17
*Sound of the Fury, The* (Faulkner), 8
Steinbeck, John
awards, 12, 14
biographical sketch, 9–12
birth, 9, 59
death, 12
education, 9–10
illnesses of, 10–11
imagination, 60
politics of, 33, 59–63, 72–73, 83

sentimentality, 33, 82–84
works by, 123
*Sweet Thursday* (Steinbeck), 10
Symbols in *Of Mice and Men*
allegory, 73–79, 90, 116
mice, 70–71, 73, 80, 105, 111, 115
rabbits, 70–71, 87, 105, 117, 120
river, 69–70
storytelling, 71

**T**

"Tennessee's Partner" (Harte), 83
*To a God Unknown* (Steinbeck), 69, 105
"To a Mountain Daisy" (Burns), 83
"To a Mouse" (Burns), 82–84
*Tortilla Flat* (Steinbeck), 10, 60, 79, 100
success of, 107–8
*Travels with Charlie: In Search of America* (Steinbeck), 12

**U**

Uncaring and impassive world theme
in *Of Mice and Men*, 49, 90–91, 94

**V**

"Vigilante, The" (Steinbeck), 61

**W**

*Wayward Bus, The* (Steinbeck), 60
setting of, 69
Wilder, Thornton, 13–14, 79
*Winter of Our Discontent* (Steinbeck), 12

**Y**

Yearning theme
in *Of Mice and Men*, 24, 85